D0049173

Where in the World Should I Invest?

AN INSIDER'S GUIDE TO MAKING MONEY AROUND THE GLOBE

Karim Rahemtulla

WILEY

John Wiley & Sons, Inc.

Published by John Wiley & Sons, Inc., Hoboken, New Jersey.
Published simultaneously in Canada.

For general information on our other products and services or for technical
support, please contact our Customer Care Department within the United States
at (800) 762-2974, outside the United States at (317) 572-3993 or fax (317)
572-4002.

Wiley also publishes its books in a variety of electronic formats. Some content that
appears in print may not be available in electronic books. For more information
about Wiley products, visit our web site at www.wiley.com.

Library of Congress Cataloging-in-Publication Data:

Rahemtulla, Karim.
    Where in the world should I invest : an insider's guide to making
money around the globe / Karim Rahemtulla.
        p. cm. — (Agora series ; 69)
    Includes index.
    ISBN 978-1-118-17191-2 (cloth); ISBN 978-1-118-22678-0 (ebk);
    ISBN 978-1-118-23990-2 (ebk); ISBN 978-1-118-26453-9 (ebk)
        1. Investments, Foreign.   2. Investments.   I. Title.
    HG4538.R24   2012
    332.67'3—dc23   2012003554

Printed in the United States of America
10 9 8 7 6

*For Isabel and Gabriela—the loves of my life.
One of life's greatest gifts is the gift of travel . . .
embrace each opportunity to do so.*

Contents

Know Where to Look

Humility is the first requirement of successful investing. We have to realize that we don't know what is going on . . . and that we certainly can't predict the future.

That means we have to find investment positions that work out even when they are based on absolute uncertainty and near complete ignorance.

Richard Russell tells us that in the film business they say that "nobody knows anything." I guess they are always surprised in Hollywood by which films are box-office successes and which aren't. Sometimes, they bet millions on a film with high expectations, only to see it flop at the box office. Then, they are surprised again when a film that they barely funded at all becomes a runaway success. Being an old hand in the movie business doesn't mean you will pick a blockbuster every time, but at least you know where to look to find them. Then, all they can do is to take educated guesses, while recognizing that they will probably be surprised.

Karim can certainly take educated guesses, too. He's been educated by roaming the world. He was born in Africa, studied in England and Canada, lives in Florida, and travels frequently. But there's more to this book than a series of educated guesses. There's also a very big idea. And the only thing that bothers me about the idea is that it is too obvious. Where's the surprise, I ask myself?

The idea is simple. The developed world is growing slowly, if at all. The emerging world—which includes all sorts of countries in all

Percent Change in Most Recent Four-Year Period for Which Data Is Available

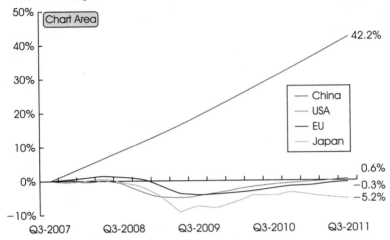

Figure F.1   GDP Growth

Source: Calculated from OECD Quarterly National Accounts and China Bureau of National Statistics, U.S. and China, 3Q 2007–3Q 2011, EU and Japan 2Q 2007–2Q 2011.

sorts of different phases of economic development—is growing more quickly. Here's a stark and simple illustration:

Figure F.1 shows what has happened over the past four years. There has been no real growth to speak of in the developed world. China is booming.

The big idea is that this process will continue. *Grosso modo.* It doesn't mean that China has to continue growing at such a sizzling pace. Or that the developed countries will necessarily stay in their slump. But if the idea is right, the developed world will continue to outperform the undeveloped world for the foreseeable future.

Why might this idea be correct? One region is developed. The other is not. It seems more likely that the undeveloped region will play catch-up than that the developed region will sprint further ahead. Catch-up is easier. It doesn't require learning any new tricks. The dogs in the undeveloped world just have to look at the dogs in the developed world and do what they do. Which is just what we've seen over the past 30 years.

The developed countries have heavy industry. So, the developing countries put up steel mills and auto plants. The developed world has shopping malls. So, they built them in the undeveloped world, too. Developed economies have highways, ports, container shipping, banks, McDonald's—and all the rest of a modern economy's infrastructure. The developing countries put them in place. The developed world appreciates the role of private property, and a court system to sort out problems, and markets to set prices and guide production. They now have those things in the developing world, too.

But the trend of faster growth in the developing countries isn't just about imitation. There is something more profound going on.

Another way to look at the growth difference between the developed world and the emerging world is as an expression of the principle of "regression to the mean." For approximately 99,700 years of human existence a man's labor in India was about as rewarding as a man's labor in Africa or Europe. It's only in the last 300 years or less that wages in Europe and its Europeanized colonies raced ahead. But I imagine there is no inherent reason why, after all this time, that one human should be more productive than another. If this is so, you could expect the abnormality to be corrected, with the wages of humans in India and Indianapolis both regressing to a mean.

But how did they get so far apart? What, exactly, was going on . . . and why might it have come to an end now?

Much of the growth and prosperity of the developed world—if not all of it—can be traced to innovations and discoveries brought online in the eighteenth and nineteenth centuries. These were two: the discovery of America and the use of fossil fuel.

When Columbus crossed the Atlantic in 1492, he was only marginally richer, more productive, and more technologically advanced than other seafarers from centuries earlier. The Chinese apparently roamed large areas of ocean. So did the Phoenicians. And the Vikings. But America is much closer to Europe than to China, and the Europeans who followed Columbus were more ready, willing, and able to take advantage of his discovery. Europeans found an almost unbelievable amount of new resources. The Iberians—Spain and Portugal—focused on what is today Latin America. The French and English directed their energy to North America. At first, the Iberians seemed to get the best of the bargain. They found money—gold and silver—which gave their economies an immediate rush. But the effect was short-lived and harmful. What they got was the equivalent of today's printing press money—an increase in the supply of money with no increase in the ability to produce things. The result was inflation and the impoverishment of the entire Iberian peninsula. To the north, the haul was similarly huge, but it was in a different form. The English and French discovered vast energy and resource wealth. They found things that they could use to create real wealth: timber for fuel, rivers that made communication easy, abundant minerals, and vast expanses of virgin farmland. It took time. It took work, saving, and investment, but the treasures of the North were ultimately transformed into much greater and much more enduring wealth. This was especially true after oil became widely used as the fuel of choice. America had a lot of it. Oil-fired machines soon increased output so greatly that the average person in America, Europe, and later in Japan, became much richer than his contemporaries in the undeveloped world.

Oil was essential. This is also why the Anglo-Saxon countries were able to hold onto their leading position for the past two centuries. They had oil. Their major challengers—Germany and Japan—did not.

But innovations are innovations. They produce growth but not eternally. You can understand why by looking quickly at the great innovations of human experience. Man is an animal. He fills the niche nature allows him. He probably lived on the African savannah for many thousands of years with no progress or growth of any kind. Then, the discovery of fire allowed him to extend his range. We imagine that there followed a growth spurt that brought him into the colder regions of Europe and Asia. He then discovered the bow and arrow, further increasing his available food supply and extending the range that nature permitted him. So, too, did the domestication of animals and the development of sedentary agriculture allow him to put more food on the table with less exertion, thereby permitting another growth spurt.

But once the new, wider niche is filled out, his progress and population growth level out and once again become stagnant. So, we have to wonder: Is the developed world at the end of its growth spurt?

In the early 1970s I recall driving from Maryland to New Mexico. For some reason, there was a price war being waged along Route 66. One station advertised gasoline at 28 cents a gallon. Another went down to 24 cents. And they washed your windshield, too.

Today, the typical person in the United States pays about 17 times as much for gasoline. Adjusted for changes in the Consumer Price Index, this individual pays about five or six times as much in real terms as he did 30 years ago. He pays much more of his income for gasoline, in other words. Why? Because the price of oil has gone up and his income hasn't.

Perhaps in Europe, the United States, and Japan the use of fossil fuels has leveled off. The number of miles driven in the United States—which have risen steadily from the day Henry Ford built the first affordable "Tin Lizzie"—has begun to decline. And economic growth, as you can see in Figure F.1, has come to an end. It appears that oil has reached its point of declining marginal utility. Further increments of energy—at today's prices—fail to produce enough additional output to justify the expense.

While the developed world's use of energy is on the decline, the emerging world can't get enough of it. The reason is self-evident. The emerging world has billions of people who don't already own all of the energy-guzzling paraphernalia of modern life. And they are acquiring the means to afford it.

Figure F.2 tells the China story. There's also Russia. Indonesia. Brazil. India. Turkey. And dozens of other high-growth emerging nations. I don't necessarily believe that any of them will become the United States of the twenty-first century. But I take it for granted that they will use a lot more oil. At present, the per capita use of oil in the United States is 10 times what it is in China. But the trend is clear: Oil use in the emerging world is rising fast . . . as you'd expect.

Of course, the other thing that is rising fast in the emerging world is personal income. This is a crucial point. In the United States, the

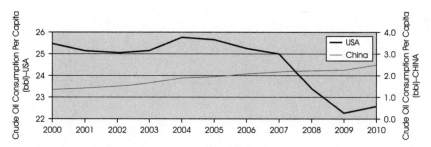

Figure F.2   China's Growing Energy Usage

Source: U.S. Energy Information Administration and U.S. Department of Energy.

typical working person reached his peak earnings-per-hour in 1974. You can argue that he gets more in social services today, such as free cheese and free pills. But that seems like small comfort when he drives up to the gas pump.

You can see the adjusted wage cost of gasoline over the past 10 years by looking at Figure F.3. The typical U.S. citizen's cost has gone up—because he isn't earning more money. The Chinese buyer finds gasoline—as a percentage of his wages—has gone down, because his earnings have increased so substantially. Chinese wages are up 281 percent over the last decade.

Even with Chinese wages up so sharply, they are still far below U.S. levels. The average worker earns roughly one-tenth as much in China as in the United States.

So, there is plenty of room for more wage growth in China. That means there is also plenty of room for more purchases of gasoline.

Many people see parallels between the rapid growth of the U.S. economy at the start of the twentieth century and the rapid growth of the Chinese economy now. They are tempted to see this as the "Chinese Century" and imagine that China will be a powerhouse, like the United States, for the next 100 years.

Yes . . . maybe . . . but . . .

The U.S. economy was a powerhouse then because it was so *unlike* what it is today. It was a free-market economy back then. Willing buyers and sellers made capital allocation decisions. Sometimes they were right. Sometimes they were wrong. But the markets corrected mistakes—continually redirecting capital from weak hands to strong

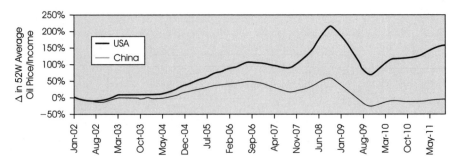

Figure F.3   Change in Crude Oil Price Divided by Change in Disposable Income—China versus United States

ones . . . and from failed projects to successful ones. Capitalism—not central planning—is how people get rich.

China is a "capitalistic" economy but with major guidance from the public sector. I don't know exactly how important those bureaucratic inputs are. I don't know if any Westerner fully grasps how it works. Even the Chinese I talk to are perplexed. But there is no question that central, regional, and local planners, by no means pure capitalists, direct vast amounts of investment capital.

As a result, there are perhaps trillions of dollars of misallocations of capital that are not readily or easily corrected. Shopping malls with no customers. Apartments with no buyers. Whole towns with no inhabitants. Many of these were built with debt. And much of that debt is bad debt.

It is impossible to predict how this will be resolved. Perhaps a blowup will be followed by a quick bounce back with reforms that allow for more sensible decision-making. Perhaps real growth is so strong that it overwhelms and smothers the mistakes. I don't know.

But that's why we need to invest as though we expect to be surprised. We surely will be.

Where the surprise will come from, I don't know. But it looks as though people in the emerging world are bound to use more oil and earn more money. And emerging markets will be better places, generally, for capital investments than the developed world.

Karim will help you figure out where to look.

BILL BONNER

Acknowledgments

My father passed away when I was relatively young. My greatest regret is his not witnessing the successes and trials of life experienced by his children, myself, my brother Minaz, and my sister Noorjehan, and, never meeting his grandchildren. But, his teachings and advice have lived on through my mother who has been a stalwart of support and great wisdom throughout my life despite the torture that I put her through as a child and teenager! This one's for you, Mom!

It began on the basketball court at Rollins College where I have been playing for more than a couple of decades with a great group of people three times a week. One of those players was Mark Skousen, editor of *Forecasts and Strategies*, and a very close friend. Mark, always seemed to be enjoying himself. He was an adjunct member of the faculty at the time, but he always spoke about "great" trips he had taken and how he loved writing about financial markets and stocks. I asked what he was talking about—what was his other job? He said he was an editor of a financial newsletter. I told him that was something I wanted to do—it really was that simple. He put me in touch with his friend Bill Bonner at Agora. Agora was a very small company then and my job was to take over the Research Director's position from Robert Czeschin, who had moved to Asia to set up shop. Little did I know that it was the beginning of the longest and best journey of my life . . . a lot of which is threaded throughout this book.

Exactly 20 years ago I flew to Baltimore to interview with Bill Bonner, the head of Agora Publishing. It was a cold winter's day and I had never been to Baltimore before. Agora's office was located in a townhouse next to a French bakery, surrounded by dilapidated buildings and across from the Projects. As I parked my car, I saw three men running across the Jones Falls Expressway, which ended close to the office. They were shooting at each other. Having just flown up from the tranquil setting of my small town, Winter Park, Florida, it was something I was not ready for.

Twenty years later, I am still with Agora and grateful for every minute I have been associated with this unique organization. Many people are surprised at the success of Agora as an organization because of what seems like a lack of a traditional corporate "feel" for such a large group. They would be less surprised if they spent a day with the founder, Bill Bonner. His willingness to allow people like myself to "write their own job description" at a very early stage, allowed for an explosion of research, ideas, information, and opinions that ultimately benefited our readers. There was room for disagreement, for argument, for opinionating, for dreaming, and for putting in motion those dreams. His door has always been open. Most have succeeded beyond their wildest expectations as part of Agora. I am one of those. It is because of the support and encouragement at various times in my career from people like Bill, Julia Guth, Addison Wiggin, Mark Ford, Sandy Franks, Deeba Jafri, Liz Fordi, Lee Euler, Chris Mayer, Paul Hollingshead, James Boric, Greg Grillot, Myles Norin, Debora Corral, Bob Compton, Danielle O'Dell, Jenny Thompson, David Melnik, Mathew Turner, Mike Geltner, Bob Williams, Mike Ward, and many, many others that this book is even possible. I do not measure my success financially, but in being able to achieve that elusive dream of really enjoying what I do everyday and having the best colleagues in the world.

I have learned that writing a book is a collaborative effort. Encouragement is needed when words are not flowing as fast. Criticism is required when mistakes or poor arguments are obvious. Most importantly, an audience is required, on a frequent basis, to prod you to write more and write better. Writing this book would have been much more difficult if not for the constant encouragement of my friend Christine Elliott O'Neal, who was relentless in her requests for the next chapter! I would like to acknowledge Lesley McIntosh, Iryna Malendevich, and Kevin Kerr for their readings of the manuscript, and their feedback . . . and to Molly Ward for her words about the cover designs. Thank you also to the fabulous faculty members at Ryde School on the Isle of Wight where I attended elementary school, Cedarbrae Collegiate Institute in Toronto where I attended high school, and Rollins College in Winter Park, Florida, where

I received both my undergraduate and graduate degrees. Many of you shaped who I am today and the lessons you taught me inside the classroom and on the court are remembered fondly daily.

This book is a journey that I wish to share with you. It explores the world that is around us from an investment and a personal perspective of someone who's "been around" it a few times. Investing globally is critical to your success as both an investor and a resident on this planet. The rest of the world *is* now you. My experiences and travels have taught me that investing overseas is both lucrative and necessary. But, investing in a foreign country, especially one that is emerging is not wise without understanding the cultural aspects of the investment. Most people focus on numbers. There is more, much, much more when it comes to putting your hard earned money at risk offshore. In the following pages I hope to take you on an unforgettable journey that leaves you wanting to both invest and learn even more!

K.R.

What You Should Know
Before You Invest

How do you identify an emerging market? On the ground, it's quite easy. The bathrooms smell, you can't drink the water, and if there's smoke in an elevator, likely you're the only one coughing. Those are the signs of opportunity!

As an investor and writer in and about emerging markets I have witnessed staggering growth prospects, some of which were realized as in the case of China, and some that failed to meet the test, especially those countries in Central America. Every "China story" has its start somewhere, and knowing where to look and the signs to look for are as important as knowing how to invest in these up-and-coming markets.

Emerging market investing is not for the faint of heart. But then, neither is investing in any market of late. Most non-emerging market investors tend to look to these opportunities as being fraught with risk. It's true. Countries that have frequent changes in leadership, high rates of poverty, illiteracy, and sometimes even high rates of crime are hardly the types of markets that engender confidence. Yet, it is precisely these markets that offer the greatest opportunity if they can fulfill their promise of a better future for their populations. Often, this is not the case. Pie in the sky projections by analysts who garner their research from the Internet or popular news media tend to paint a rosier picture than is actually the case. Worse, they sometimes paint a picture that is far more negative than it should be.

In this book I have tried my best to paint a candid picture. The picture I want you to see is one that comes from someone who has been on the ground, met with local officials at the lowest and highest levels, and dealt with frauds and phonies, finance ministers, and soon-to-be-deposed finance ministers. There is nothing conventional about investing in emerging markets, but that does not mean there are not opportunities that arise out of the lack of convention. In fact, it is the lack of a guidebook and the lack of convention that provides opportunity for those who are willing to seek it out. If it were as easy as investing in a sure thing, like China, then there would be far more millionaires on the planet than there are. Yet, even with the obvious growth in places like China, India, Brazil, Chile, and South Africa, investors have yet to cash in en masse. For the most part, they lack tools, a guide, and confidence.

In the following pages I have provided that elusive guidebook to emerging markets, the unvarnished truth so to speak. It's a viewpoint from someone who set the rose-colored glasses aside almost 20 years ago when he encountered his first taste of Chinese hooch at a steel mill purportedly owned by a private company. As it turns out, this steel mill was anything but legitimate and the owners were engaged in massive fraud, one that is still being perpetrated in many Chinese companies today as any who have been following the business media can attest to. But, for every suspect opportunity there lie 10 more that are legitimate, undercovered, and waiting for that fortunate investor who has taken the time to look, learn, and deploy capital at a very early stage. Cambodia and Vietnam are excellent examples of frontier markets that will likely deliver outsized returns in the years ahead, something I delve into in some depth in the chapters ahead.

Emerging markets share many common characteristics. They usually have poor tax collection systems if any, poor infrastructure for transportation of goods and people, lack of codified securities laws, nonexistent title verification, poor adjudication processes, and sometimes-incomprehensible laws regarding foreign investment. Yet, these are not issues that have dissuaded investors like the late John Templeton or Mark Mobius from making fortunes for themselves and their investors/followers in the past three decades. All of these problems create cheap opportunities and should be viewed in a positive light. If everything ran like it did in the West, then emerging markets would be priced in similar fashion, and the profit motive would disappear for investors. Problems exist, but as they are solved, the result is greater returns for those who know the difference between growing pains and systemic issues. When investing in emerging markets one often has to hold his nose both on the ground and in his portfolio. There will never be that same comfort level of full and accurate disclosure or Western accounting standards or transparency. In fact, it is a hallmark of emerging markets that transparency is less than clear. If these markets were as easy to decipher as those in the West, they would likely not be considered emerging markets anymore.

The opportunity lies in cutting through the bullshit and looking past the smokescreens. That can only be done with an understanding of what makes an emerging market viable for enough time that it can transition into a developed market. Many, like Turkey, are on that cusp. Others, like Thailand, will remain emerging markets forever. Some, like those of the former Soviet Union, may actually regress and become closed or impossible to invest in altogether. What you need to look for is trends. And these are not only market trends, but also political trends, economic trends, trends in taxation, trends in accounting transparency, and finally, trends in spending.

Once you think that you understand how emerging markets work and which ones are likely to succeed or fail, your job is only half complete. The next step is to understand and figure out how to actually invest in and profit from your knowledge. Emerging markets are traders' markets. They do not follow a "buy and hold" script. By their nature, they are volatile and unpredictable. This unpredictability creates a wealth of opportunity and profits for the prepared investor. The phrase coined by Baron Rothschild in the eighteenth century, "The time to buy is when blood is in the streets," is one that should be followed religiously when dealing in emerging markets, sometimes literally. Thailand is a great example of a market that should be bought during a military coup . . . the bloodier the better. However, the phrase refers more often today to the opportunities that arise when there is massive uncertainty or panic.

I remember vividly sitting on my bed in the Regent Hotel in Hong Kong when I was there for the ceremony that handed Hong Kong back to the Chinese. It was July 1997. A news flash scrolled across the screen announcing that the Thai baht was collapsing. It was the beginning of the Asian financial crisis, which decimated many Asian markets. Some stocks lost 60 to 70 percent of their value overnight as panicked investors bailed out. Buyers who stepped in to the chaos multiplied their wealth several times over in a matter of months as the crisis subsided and plans were put forth to restabilize and recapitalize the region.

Today, emerging markets are where the growth is, plain and simple. Places like China, South Africa, Brazil, and India are growing at four to five times the rate of developed markets like the United States or Europe. In light of the recent crises that have plunged the West into the throes of recession, emerging markets present an even more compelling opportunity. The Asian financial crisis of 1997 decimated emerging markets worldwide but also forced them to pay attention to credit growth and easy money policies resulting in a more fiscally responsible environment for investors. Population growth, more disposable income, and greater foreign direct investment have created a vibrant atmosphere for growth. The emergence of China as an economic superpower has turbocharged growth prospects for all emerging markets as China has become a significant consumer of raw materials and a major manufacturing subcontractor for its smaller neighbors. Technology-driven demand has augmented growth in many markets by providing easy-to-use instant communications technology, negating the need for heavy spending on a telecommunications infrastructure and improving communications with more remote population centers that are a major source for cheap labor.

Looking forward, you have a choice. Do you continue to keep your money in a low-growth environment where an aging population saps resources and forces increasingly higher tax rates, or do you migrate some of your capital to markets that have decades of growth ahead of them. The answer should be quite simple. And now, with the ability to easily invest across borders, a major barrier to investing offshore in emerging markets has also been lifted.

Information flows are freer, more accurate, and more accessible thanks to the Internet. Money flows are also easier thanks to foreign brokers who are eager to facilitate trades. And, foreign governments are loosening up restrictions for foreign investors in a bid to attract more capital to finance growth. The age of the emerging market has only just begun, and this is one ride you can't afford to miss.

1

Journeys to China

In the summer of 2011, one of the most successful hedge fund managers of the century, John Paulson, made a bet that allegedly cost him and his investors $500 million in a matter of months. It wasn't on some wrong-way bet on the options market or a commodities trade gone sour. If that were the case, it would be understandable because of the risks involved. No, it was a loss on the shares of a company called Sino-Forest (TRE.T). The company, as the name implies, was a Chinese company involved in the forestry business. A sound bet, it would seem, thanks to the booming market for commodities in China. Better still, the company's shares were listed not on some obscure exchange in Ulan Bator, but rather they were listed on a major Canadian exchange.

On March 31, 2011, the shares of Sino-Forest reached their high at $25.85. On June 21, 2011, the shares closed at $1.99. In the period between, a company that specializes in researching short-sale opportunities, Muddy Waters, released a report questioning the veracity of the claims that Sino-Forest had made regarding its land holdings. Here's what the founder of Muddy Waters, Carson Block, had to say about Sino-Forest:

> It's a Ponzi scheme in that the company perpetually issues securities in order to fund itself. Even by its own fraudulent numbers, the company does not generate any free cash and has not done so in 16 years. Were the company unable to issue additional securities to fund itself, it would collapse. That, to me,

is the definition or epitomizes the definition of a Ponzi. In this situation, the company appears to be investing for the twenty-third century. It's 16 straight years burning cash, no guidance as to what the rationale is to acquire so many trees so far ahead of customer orders. This is taking a capex fraud—we have found several of these in China—it's taking it to the next level where you're not constrained by the walls of a factory and no one is able to really see the movement of physical goods. It could grow to be infinite provided that the capital markets continue to fund it.

Now, whether Mr. Block was right is really not the point. The fact that one of the biggest and most influential fund managers in the world miscalculated on such a big stage is. Had Mr. Paulson consulted with me . . . or read what I had written after my first trip to China back in the early 1990s, it might have saved him and his investors a few hundred million dollars.

The First Journey: Wolong YuYe

My first journey to China, about 17 years ago now, was courtesy of an all-expenses-paid research trip funded by an investment group out of Florida. The outfit wanted me and a gaggle of other editors to provide some coverage of the "China story." Yes, my friends, China was a story then, as well.

This was before the Asian financial crisis, when Chinese companies were going public in their local markets with the help of some shady Hong Kong business types. Hong Kong, if you were not aware, was born of illicit trade . . . and it hasn't changed since birth. It's just cleaner, smells better, and you now can say thanks in English before getting ripped off.

As my plane landed in Chengdu, in the Sichuan Province, I noticed that it was quite dark outside. I am more used to seeing the street light grids that illuminate most U.S. cities when I travel. There was not a single light in sight. It's hard to be all lit up when you don't have electricity in the rural areas. We landed. As we walked through the customs and immigration lines, I noticed that one of the agents had pulled over a cadre of Japanese businessmen and was giving them a good amount of grief. I guess old memories die hard in China.

The first thing I noticed outside the terminal was a huge sign for Jeep Cherokee—remember, this was circa 1995. A huge Mercedes pulled up and whisked us to our hotel, the Jin Jiang. I was beginning to get the feeling that China had really come of age. The hotel was arguably the best hotel I have ever stayed in, five-star all the way. Satellite TV, electric blinds, marble baths—these guys really knew how to live.

Tour of the Steel Mill

The next morning, I was ready for the tour of the steel mill that we were scheduled to visit. The mill used to be owned by the state but was now privatized and owned by a Hong Kong-listed company. Bicycles—I have never seen so many. Cars? I have never seen so few. As we navigated through crowded streets, it was apparent that China would have to do a lot more than a few hundred billion dollars in trade to get up to speed as a first-world country. All around us, poverty made its sometimes pungent presence known fully and completely. A chicken in every pot? How about just a pot first?

We reached the steel mill and were greeted by a huge turnout of employees and staff all wearing their Sunday best and smiling. They could smell the profits reeking from our first-world clothes. The Chinese had a weird sense of fashion. The up and comers wore Western suits—with the labels still showing—the sign of prosperity. We were led around the factory, given a tour of the smelter, offered bamboo hard hats (I still have mine), and warned about the dangerous environment. Apparently the amputees had the day off for this tour.

As we toured the facility, many of the upper-level executives who spoke very good English began to cozy up with us. The plant was spectacular, no? It was now the lowest-cost producer of steel in China—ever since the state let go. We were now on our way to see the local Communist Party head who agreed to give a little speech to mark our visit. We entered a building that was set up like a small amphitheater. The officials welcomed us with smiles and nods. I held on tight to my wallet. The head official said nothing of significance or worth remembering. But as he wiped his hair back, I noticed that he was wearing a real Rolex watch. (As a one-time watch enthusiast, I can spot the real thing from a mile away—it's all in the magnification.) I asked myself how a Communist Party official could afford such a luxury on barely $20 a month for a salary. Then I remembered that I asked myself the same questions in 1982 when I visited Russia as a younger, more naïve man. He must have gotten rid of the manila envelope by now.

The meeting ended. We were invited to a party with the party. At the party, the officials and executives were getting very friendly and anxious. They began extolling the virtues of the steel mill, its huge profitability, and the capitalist changes taking place in China. No one was biting. They loosened their ties and announced that it was time for some Wolong Yuye (not to be confused with Falun Gong). It was barely 2 P.M. and out of nowhere appeared a bevy of beauties with bottles and glasses. The beauties, as I learned later, were also a freebie. Wolong Yuye is the Chinese equivalent of moonshine . . . I guess. I don't drink alcohol (before 6 P.M. anyway) and so I declined to partake in this party with the party.

Pulling a Fast One

These Chinese were not shy about demonstrating their fondness for hooch. It was too late. An hour had passed and I was the only sober one in the room, probably in the entire plant. They started to spill their guts—figuratively. The plant was not owned by the Hong Kong company. It was still owned by the state . . . ha ha. The company executives in cahoots with Mr. Rolex had leased the plant to the Hong Kong company so they could pitch it to unsuspecting foreigners (read Americans who love a bargain) and then turn over their shares in the public company at a nice profit. If a few of the analysts and writers on the trip wrote about this Hong Kong small cap that also traded on the NASDAQ bulletin boards, their retirement would be set in stone, or better yet, U.S. dollars. Then, they could tear up the lease agreement and the state would be none the wiser.

The Second Journey: This Time It's Different

The trip ended badly in more ways than one. I left feeling that I had wasted my time. I came to the conclusion that the only people who would make money in China then were the Chinese. If you want to invest in China, be careful and look to experience.

John Paulson learned this lesson the hard way, as have many other investors over the years. Emerging markets offer a bounty of profits to investors, but most don't understand the inner workings or subtle cultural nuances that permeate every facet of investing in these markets. Being early is good; being right is better. Over the past 20-odd years I have visited, invested in, made money from, and lost money in many of the emerging markets that you are just beginning to read about in the financial press today.

There is money to be made, lots of it. But, making that money requires a better understanding of how these markets work, which markets work better than others, and where you can safely trade individual stocks in these markets. It all begins, though, with an understanding of the people and culture that you are investing in and with.

The China Experiment

China is on everybody's mind, as it should be. It is the single most important country for investors and non-investors alike in this century. As a burgeoning economic superpower it holds the key to growth in Asia. As a military superpower it threatens the world with its shrouded intentions. As an ideological superpower it can act in a manner that is often misunderstood by the West but clearly understood by its neighbors.

I'll begin my journey in Chengdu in the mid-1990s. As I spoke about in my introduction, it was a rude awakening from an investing standpoint. I arrived in China at a fairly early stage in its most recent growth spurt. I doubt that Chengdu today looks anything like it did just 16 years ago. The place was so polluted, I could barely see across the street. An industrial city, Chengdu is also the capital of China's Sichuan Province and one of the country's largest manufacturing centers.

On the main street people rode on bicycles as far as the eye could see. There were probably more bikes on that one street than in the whole of Amsterdam. There were no cars to speak of. Like worker bees, people rode to work at factories and steel mills early in the morning. All were dressed in the same gray, drab mandarin-collared Mao suits. I could barely discern male from female. On each corner an old woman wearing a Chinese cone field hat would be sweeping the sidewalk with a primitive bamboo sweep, moving the dust from sidewalk to street, only to return later and do the same again—probably with the same dust.

As I walked through the side streets of the hutongs, old men would be playing Weiqi or Mahjong while puffing on their cigarettes. Everyone smoked, adding to the already squalid air. There was little worth buying from street vendors, because there was not much for sale. Chengdu was not Shanghai. And, at that time, Chinese consumers barely had a pot to piss in, let alone extra cash to buy niceties.

But, there were great bargains to be had at state-owned shops. At the time, the renminbi was trading at just over 8 to 1 versus the U.S. dollar (compared to 6.4 to 1 today—see Figure 1.1) and the only place selling authentic treasures such as scrolls and paintings were the two-story government shops where there was no bargaining, no credit cards, and no toilet paper. All in all, it was a depressing place.

My visit to Chengdu and my meetings with the steel mill executives left me with a bad taste about China. Worse, I lost

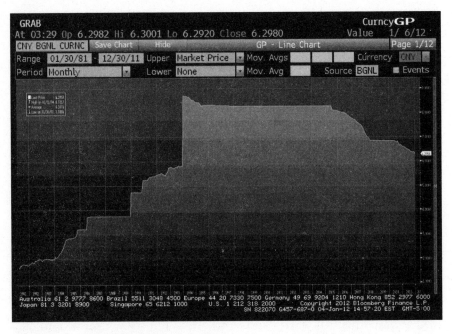

Figure 1.1 USDCNY Exchange Rate

10 pounds on the trip because the food was unrecognizable at worst and inedible at best, unless sliced bull testicles appeal to your palate. It was a white rice trip. There were no McDonald's restaurants in Chengdu, no Kentucky Fried Chickens, and nothing that even resembled something I would like to eat. I survived on white rice and the excellent western breakfast buffet at the Jin Jiang. On my return home, everything in my suitcase, and the suitcase itself, had a distinct odor . . . it took me several trips to learn that it was a combination of green tea and mushrooms, neither of which I consumed!

The Third Trip: Fast Forward

In 1997 I made my third trip to China, well kind of. I landed in Great Britain, but departed from China, without traveling more than a dozen miles in between. It was July 1997 and I was in Hong Kong for the handover ceremonies, China's "coming out" party. The Brits were leaving and handing the keys to arguably the most prosperous city in China back to the Chinese. The city was painted red from head to toe. It was a miserable four days. Monsoon rains drenched the place. From my window at the Regent, I was supposed to be able to see the harbor. I could see nothing but droplets of water on the glass. The entire trip was spent shopping at stalls and markets while waiting for the ceremonies to take place. Most of Hong Kong was on holiday, and because the real purpose of the trip was to explore India, Hong Kong was just a timely stopover. It was exciting, however, as the Asian financial crisis was just beginning with the collapse of Thailand's economy and the Thai baht starting to make headlines.

The night of the handover ceremonies was no different than any of the preceding nights. Perched atop the stock exchange building we waited for all the pomp and circumstance to begin in the harbor. Remember the stories you heard about the Chinese trying to control the weather? Well, let me tell you that during the two-hour-long ceremony the skies cleared and the fireworks display went off without a hitch. Within minutes of the actual handover ceremonies ending, the skies opened up and it rained for the rest of the trip.

At the time of the handover and during the months preceding it, there was easy money to be made in the Chinese market.

Exuberant Chinese and foreigners alike were pumping money into Hong Kong and China stocks en masse.

Earlier in the year, however, there were signs of a top. New World Development Co. set a record with its $92 million purchase of a home atop Hong Kong island for redevelopment. Property bubbles often precede stock market crashes, as those in Japan and the United States are acutely aware.

I remember writing about it and recommending that my readers buy China and sell after the handover. I was right, but not for the reasons I thought. The handover coincided with the Asian financial crisis, and that was among the leading reasons that the Hong Kong and Chinese markets cratered so quickly after the event. They plunged but not for very long. What happened next is of note.

After the Hong Kong market began to crumble under the weight of margin, real estate speculation gone sour, and the domino effect of the Asian crisis, the government of Hong Kong, under the auspices of the mainland government, began to overtly buy shares on the market, crushing short sellers. At one point the government bought more than 10 percent of banking giant HSBC shares in an

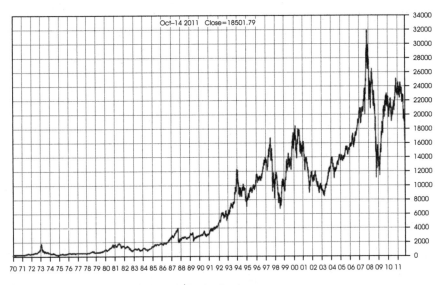

Figure 1.2   Hong Kong Hang Seng Index

Source: www.sharelynx.com.

effort to quell the tide of sellers. It worked, but at what price? After spending at least $15 billion—a mammoth amount at the time—the government had convinced me, at least, that it would do anything to prevent a collapse or make sure that any collapse would be quite short-lived. The price for taking risks was not failure but government support. It's a lesson that played out again in the U.S. financial crisis of 2008 to 2009. It also meant that valuing companies in the market was next to impossible during a crisis. More importantly, it set the precedent for how to trade emerging market shares, something I will talk about in more depth in a later chapter.

What I will miss most about the Hong Kong of 1997 was flying into the airport sideways on a 747 and almost being able to read the names on the designer labels of the clothes hanging to dry on the balconies. It's an experience that will never be repeated, as the Kai Tak Airport ceased operations in 1998 to make way for the new Chek Lap Kok Airport that was built on reclaimed land.

The ETF Effect

Up until the early 2000s, there were few ways to invest in China comfortably. One of the most popular vehicles was closed-end funds. These funds operate similarly to mutual funds with respect to the fact that they hold a variety of investments in a particular sector or country. For a place like China, it was next to impossible for an individual investor to buy shares or other types of investments in anything other than a few of the "red chip" names. The problem with this is that most of these big name stocks had already been bid up by investors who didn't take time to explore the other possibilities.

The big difference between closed-end funds and mutual funds is the way they trade. Closed-end funds issue shares that trade on an exchange. The share price is initially set based on the net asset value (NAV) of the underlying holdings. Mutual funds are priced the same way, but they do not trade during the day on an exchange and their prices are reset once each day for buyers and sellers. They also issue as many shares as needed on a continuous basis based on supply and demand. The price of a mutual fund reflects the value of the holdings every day and that is the basis for the price. These last two points are important.

Closed-end funds, by virtue of their real-time trading and their fixed number of issued shares, are subject to the whims of the market and supply and demand. This results in an unusual and unusually profitable way of playing the Chinese markets, or any markets for that matter, even today.

Closed-end funds trade at either a discount or a premium to NAV. If the shares trade at a level higher than the value of the holdings, that is a premium. If they trade at a level lower than the value of the holdings, that is a discount. This allows for some massive opportunities for the savvy investor. All of these closed-end funds have historical data that show the premium or discount they trade for. In the case of emerging markets it depends on how well the underlying market is performing. If it is doing well, the funds trade at premiums. If poorly, then discounts. Not exactly rocket science.

There have been many occasions during which you could have (and I did) purchased closed-end funds at discounts ranging from 10 to 35 percent off NAV. That's like buy one dollar's worth of investments for 65 to 90 cents. How can this situation exist?

Because closed-end funds trade like stocks in the market during the day, they are subject to investor supply and demand. During the Asian financial crisis, closed-end funds were pummeled as investors flocked out of them in droves. There is only one market mechanism to prevent an oversupply of shares during a panic: lower prices until equilibrium between buyers and sellers is once again achieved. The crisis lasted for months and during those months it was possible to buy closed-end funds at discounts of more than 25 percent. Within a couple of years, those discounts became premiums once again. It doesn't take balls of steel to make these investments, just a better understanding of why and when these opportunities present themselves. One of my favorite trading vehicles for China during times of crisis is still the Templeton Dragon Fund (NYSE:TDF) managed by Mark Mobius, a veteran trader of Asian companies.

A glance at the price chart of the fund (Figure 1.3) reflects major inflection points in the emerging markets. Take a look at how many opportunities you might have had in the past 15 years to double, triple, and even quadruple your money time and again. The secret is patience. If there are two common themes among

Figure 1.3   Templeton Dragon Fund

emerging markets, it is that they are eminently tradable and prone to crisis.

Finding Bargains

There is one website in particular that I keep an eye on when I want to know when to buy and when to sell closed-end funds. It is www.closed-endfunds.com/. On this site you can type in the symbol of the fund you are following, TDF, for example. It will pull up all the pertinent information. You want to zero in on one line: the premium or discount line. There, it will tell you whether the fund is a buy or not a buy. It will tell you this by the amount of discount the fund's share price is trading to NAV. Here is my rule of thumb. If the discount to NAV is 25 percent or more, buy. When the premium reaches 10 percent or more it's time to sell. This trade can be replicated over and over again. There are two funds in particular where I employ this strategy. First, the Templeton Dragon

Fund and second the Templeton Russia and Eastern Europe Fund (NYSE:TRF). I will talk more about Russia and Eastern Europe in the coming pages.

In Figure 1.4 you can see the repetitive nature of closed-end fund behavior during periods of crisis. I took two periods and isolated them for you. The first was during the Asian financial crisis and the period that followed. The second was during the global financial crisis in 2008 and 2009 after the housing bust in the United States. As you can clearly see, the opportunities for fast profits from emerging markets are not hard to achieve if you have even some modicum of patience and knowledge about which vehicles to use. As an aside, both the U.S. crisis and the Asian crisis followed a similar track. They both occurred after a long period of easy money due to low interest rates. If you are looking for a reason for bubbles to form, easy money is the biggest one that I have encountered. As for timing entry . . . well, that is easy as well. Wait for that

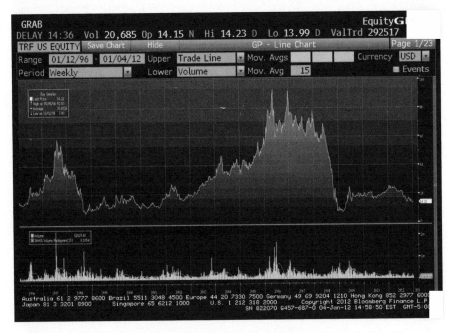

Figure 1.4   Templeton Russia and East Europe

25 percent number to kick in; better still, average your buys into these funds starting at a 25 percent discount and adding incrementally with each subsequent 5 percent discount. As yet, I have never seen a 45 percent discount.

The Two Towers

Shanghai and Beijing: two more different cities could not exist on this planet. That they are both in the same country is a source of constant amazement to me. In Shanghai you feel as if you are in a western metropolis, while Beijing appears a staid, buttoned up, traditional city. Of course, history has a lot to do with this.

Shanghai has always been the bad boy of the Orient. A city built on the fortunes of opium, strong European influence, and the morals of a drunken sailor, Shanghai is a city where anything goes . . . and often does. Shanghai is the China that fools you into thinking that China is an open, capitalist country with unlimited potential. I have to say, the place is a blast and a half but as expensive as any western city.

Beijing, on the other hand, is the center of Red China. Tiananmen Square is crawling with tourists and soldiers alike. A massive picture of Mao hangs at the entrance to the Forbidden City. Not once have I seen a picture of Mao in Shanghai. Mao's mausoleum sits in the center of the square. Beijing is China's capital city; the place where secret ambitions are fostered; where policy is formulated; where the brain trust issues edicts on everything from population control, Internet accessibility, and price controls. It is the heart of China and while it cannot hold a candle to Shanghai and its modernity and riches, Beijing calls the shots.

The Center of the World

My first visit to Beijing was in the 1990s. The airport was old, no Jetways to the plane, bicycles still outnumbered cars, and few if any cranes were on the horizon. The ride from the airport to the city center took less than half an hour. Today, a trip into town will take at least an hour, and that's if traffic cooperates!

A note about getting around in China: There is a train that you can take from the airport, but for some unexplainable reason, you have to make a couple of changes in order to get to the city center—avoid it. Take a taxi for somewhere between $25 and $30 or take a bus for less than half of that. Arranging private transportation is easy, but you will be paying western rates. If anyone speaks English, they do a great job in not revealing that fact. Always carry around your destination information in Chinese—this is a must. Cab drivers are honest for the most part (much more so than in Athens or Istanbul), and taxis are both cheap and metered.

There are six fully connected ring roads, beltways that make their way around the city. On my first visit just two were fully connected. Cranes are the national bird here and they come in one color—yellow—and they're mechanical. As far as the eye can see, in just about any city you visit there are cranes. On a recent trip from **Xian** Airport, I counted more than 100 cranes off the highway, and **that was** in poor visibility that only allowed me about 300 yards of clear sight.

Today, Beijing is one big traffic jam. There is a pecking order of cars. Volkswagens are popular, but Audis rule the roost. Most, if not all, are chauffeur driven and black. Once in a while you'll spot a Rolls Royce. It's a far cry from the days of the bicycle. Getting around town is very easy, but you need to leave lots of time. Rush hour begins around 6 A.M. and lasts until 6 P.M.—that's just the way it is. While China as a whole has spent billions on infrastructure, it just cannot keep up with the growth of automobile traffic. The casualty is time.

Most visitors to Beijing do not come here to do business. They come to see the sights and to experience Chinese history. In this respect, Beijing does not disappoint. The Forbidden City, the center of the world for the Chinese, is a fabulous complex that is relatively well preserved. It was the seat of power for the Middle Kingdom for centuries. Inside this complex there are thousands of buildings—some small and some very large. Not many buildings are open to the public, probably because they are in need of restoration. The ones that are have rooms roped off from visitor traffic. Some of the antiquities are on display, but many pieces were taken to Taiwan when Chiang Kai-shek fled the mainland in 1950 after the Communist rebellion. He ruled Taiwan until his death in 1975.

Following his departure to Taiwan, China transformed into the world's largest Communist country, led by Mao Zedong, the chairman. It was likely the low point of U.S.–Chinese relations. In fact, Mao believed strongly that Chiang Kai-shek was nothing more than a puppet for the western imperialists. Here is an excerpt from the third paragraph of his opening address on September 21 at the first plenary session of the Chinese People's Political Consultative Conference:

> In a little more than three years the heroic Chinese People's Liberation Army, an army such as the world has seldom seen, crushed all the offensives launched by the several million troops of the U.S.-supported reactionary Kuomintang government and turned to the counteroffensive and the offensive.

Old feelings die hard. Like the Japanese, toward whom the Chinese harbor the most hatred, the United States is by no means considered a friend. China has had to play the role of unwilling partner to the United States at the economic dance in order to accelerate its growth from third-world status. It has lost face each time the United States has shown support for Taiwan and for the Dalai Lama who they believe is trying to destabilize the "autonomous region" of Tibet.

As a consequence of this forced marriage between the United States and China on economic grounds, there has been a thaw in relations over the past two decades with the Chinese doing fewer bad things, publicly anyway, and the United States adopting a less critical stance toward violations of human rights, environmental policy, and trade. This marriage will not last forever, and the fallout could be devastating.

Many have asked me about China's vast holdings of U.S. Treasury securities and the impact they could have on the U.S. economy and population if the Chinese decided to dump their holdings and diversify outside the U.S. dollar. It's a valid concern, but one that really would not be in China's best interest. China has made a sort of deal with the devil and it is more vulnerable at this point than is the United States.

To understand how the two countries came to be in this unusual, somewhat symbiotic position, one must look at global dynamics. The United States is the world's wealthiest country by far. It has a culture of consumption. We buy any and everything—whether we need it or not. Buying American-made goods means spending more money. Sweat is more expensive in the United States. In China, sweat is cheap, plentiful, and easily controlled. With a one-party system that is not concerned about how it appears to the rest of the world, it is easy to mobilize a massive workforce to toil in gigantic factories for a pittance, as long as that pittance is still more than the population is used to earning.

So, China became the world's factory. It produced goods at prices that were, and still are, incredibly cheap. Quality was not a concern. The West, especially the United States, bought these goods and by doing so held down price inflation. This low inflation in the price of goods benefited the West tremendously—especially the United States, which has seen a stagnation of wage growth for the middle and lower classes for more than two decades in real terms. So, Americans could buy more stuff and feel like their standard of living was not declining as measured by the number of TV sets, pieces of furniture, and knick-knacks they accumulated.

The problem for China was that in order to fully mobilize, it had to take in foreign currency at any cost. The yuan or remnimbi (the Chinese currency) is not convertible. So, to buy things like natural resources, the Chinese had to use the single currency that is accepted by all: the U.S. dollar. At the time this began, the euro was nonexistent. The Chinese also needed to accumulate U.S. dollars because they knew that the U.S. dollar, as reserve currency, would not be subject to default fears (even though the events in 2011 surrounding the debt default fiasco must have made many in Beijing worry just a little).

Today, the U.S. dollar is accepted willingly in many places in China, especially the bigger cities and definitely the markets. In fact, I make it a point when I travel to carry a lot of small U.S. bills: $1s, $5s, and $10s. They are not only accepted, but they are not susceptible to counterfeiting, as is the Chinese yuan, especially the 100-yuan note. I found this out the hard way; fortunately the 100-yuan note was worth only about $12.50 at the time. Counterfeiting in China is not just an isolated thing; it's a way of life.

I was staying at the Grand Hyatt in Beijing. It was 2006. There was a cash machine in the lobby, and I went to withdraw some local currency—about 1,000 yuan. Out came 10 crisp 100-yuan notes. Knowing that I would need small bills for the street I went to the hotel cashier to get some change. She politely informed me that three of my bills, which had come out of the hotel's own ATM right in front of her, were fake and that she could do nothing about it. That, my friend, is brazen counterfeiting!

In the mid-2000s, China pretended to bow under the pressure of Western criticism of its counterfeit industry. Prior to around 2006, on the streets of any city, you could openly buy any knock-off that you could dream of. Louis Vuitton, Gucci, Rolex, Cartier, Chanel—these are the favorites. For $12 you could easily add a beautiful Chanel knockoff to your collection. The quality would surprise you. I was in the old market in Shanghai recently and I didn't see one knockoff purse anywhere. For a moment I thought the Chinese were actually taking it seriously.

Within five minutes, a well-dressed gentleman carrying a spiral binder approached me. He insisted, as is always the case, on showing me the contents. I really enjoy being bothered by the locals—it gives me a much better feel for what is happening at the street level. His binder was stuffed with high-quality, color laminate pages listing every model number of every purse from every designer imaginable. If I were interested, he would take me to see the actual purses and luggage. I was, and off we went. We walked through a series of narrow alleyways behind the market (yes, it was a little scary) until we reached a modest little home. The door opened and inside were a few family members enjoying tea and a couple of for-eigners looking at the wares. What he showed me next astounded me. He opened a door to a room that had ceilings at least 20 feet high and each shelf from floor to ceiling was packed with merchan-dise. Mont Blanc briefcases, Louis Vuitton suitcases, even brands such as Tumi and Samsonite were being knocked off. And, the prices . . . well, that's worth another story.

How to Bargain in China

Know this: if you walk away from a vendor in China without any merchandise, it will be a rare event indeed. Bargaining with the Chinese is fun, exciting, and a game of sorts. There is no ill will, and they know that for every 1 hard bargainer there will be 10 who will reward them bountifully. I am that one. When I first visited China there was not much to buy, let alone bargain for. In subsequent trips it has been one shopping spree after another. On one trip I bought a designer suitcase for $10. As I got on the coach I noticed that a fellow traveler had the same suitcase. I inquired. She paid $120. I said nothing. She was happy as a lark. The same suitcase, real of course, retailed for more than $1,000 in the United States.

The difference today versus just 10 years ago is the Internet. It's no secret that you can't log onto Facebook or YouTube in China (well that's not true either . . . if you are on a virtual private network you can get on just fine). You can however, log onto just about every other site and that means access to information about pricing. On my second trip a woman was trying her hardest to sell me a fake Rolex. I told her I wasn't interested. At one point she asked me a very surprising question. She asked me why we Westerners were so enamored of this brand. She had no idea what she was selling. I pointed to a colleague who was wearing a real Rolex. I had already gotten her down to around 10 yuan or about $1.50 for one that one of my friends wanted to buy. Her cost was probably around 50 or 75 cents. I told her that the real Rolex that my colleague was wearing—it was a Presidents model—sold for about 160,000 yuan in the United States. Her jaw dropped. That was more money than she would see in her lifetime. She understood. And, now the majority of Chinese market vendors do, as well. Today it is much harder to get a great deal because so many people are online checking out prices for the real things—they are more informed, more educated, and make better margins! Good deals? They're still a dime a dozen. If you are looking for goods and services, China is cheap. If you want a great meal or hotel room, you'll pay U.S. prices.

In Beijing the place to score great bargains, with lots of selection, is a place called the Pearl Market. Yes, they sell pearls, lots of them. A gorgeous 10-millimeter strand will set you back between $30 and $70. But, they sell more than pearls in China, much more. I buy all of my eyeglasses there. For around $40 I can get a pair of rimless glasses, scratch resistant, with reflective coating . . . ready in less than one hour. In the United States it would be $300 and two weeks. You can buy anything in the Pearl Market—glasses, purses, electronics, T-shirts, designer clothing, jewelry—and you have five stories' worth of shops to choose from. The higher you go, the better the quality. After one visit, you will have a very difficult time ever shopping at home, especially for precious and semiprecious stones. One necklace that a friend bought cost $20. I saw the identical one at a gallery in the United States for $400— identical! It's worth going to China just for the shopping—it will pay for the entire trip and more. It's also why there is absolutely no hope for any Western country to compete when it comes to manufacturing. Quality is an issue, but if you pay more you can get that in China as well, and it will still cost a third or less than in any western country. It's about sweat—in China it's cheap . . . for now.

There are a lot of places to shop in Beijing, street stalls and so on, but, I found the Pearl Market (16 Hongqiao Lu, Beijing, China, 010-6711-7429) to have pretty much everything in one place and it's quite safe and a lot of fun. It's also air-conditioned for those hot summer days. It's only about a $3 cab ride from most places in the city center—just remember to take your hotel information in Chinese for the ride back!

The Great Wall

Without a doubt this is one of the wonders of the world—and the longest to boot. Beijing is a perfect staging point for visiting sections of the Wall. The section at Badaling is probably the closest and one of the best preserved. Be aware, the Wall is not for sissies. You will never get your mind around the amount of work, resources, and loss of life that it probably took to build the Great Wall. It snakes—over hills and mountains and its remnants can be found over a 3,000-mile stretch—imagine a massive wall from New York to Los Angeles!

The best time to visit is in the spring when the wildflowers are blooming on the hillsides, and when it's cooler. Beijing is oppressively hot in the summer and tourists begin flocking to the Wall in droves starting in mid-May. The winter is also a great time to see the Wall, but be forewarned, Beijing is cold in the winter and snow is not uncommon.

The Wall was constructed to keep invaders out of China and probably as a huge exercise in ego building. The steps of the Wall are not even. Let me explain. The risers can range from 2 to 14 inches and do so in very random order. It will cause a lot of lactic acid buildup in the thighs just to scale a small portion. If it's wet, it'll be slippery and very hard to climb. If you're going to climb the Wall, do it only if you are physically fit. You will likely run out of breath after a few hundred steps. The Wall at Badaling is about an hour and a half from the Forbidden City, and there is little on the way or out there except for a few souvenir stands. Be sure to eat well before your trip!

The Wall and the Forbidden City are two must-sees when you go to China . . . there are few such spectacular man-made structures in the world.

Badaling Great Wall/Great Wall of Badaling Section

Admission fee: CNY 45 (4/1 to 10/31); CNY 40 (11/1 to 3/31)

Cable car: CNY 40 (one way); CNY 60 (roundtrip)

Hours: 06:40 to 18:30

Entrance fee: RMB40 (11/1 to 3/31); RMB 45 (4/1 to 10/31)

Time needed to visit: One and a half hours

The Forbidden City

Admission fee: RMB40 in the off season (11/1 to 3/31), RMB60 in the peak season (4/1 to 10/31).

Hours: Oct.16 to April 31: 8:30 to 16:30. Latest time for ticket purchase: 15:30 April 16 to Oct.15: 8:30 to 17:00. Latest time for ticket purchase: 16:00.

Note: The prime area for sightseeing is the center area of the Imperial Palace, however, if time permits, you could also have a walk and visit the west areas.

The Real Pearl of the Orient

At the Long Bar in Shanghai's Waldorf Astoria you can kick back and enjoy a great cigar and possibly the best burger in town. In China everything has history. In Shanghai, that history has always been intertwined with trade, legal and illegal. Shanghai sits on the eastern coast of China at the mouth of the Yangtze River. A port city, Shanghai was the hub for Chinese commerce with the outside world. The city experienced a decline in fortune during communist rule, but after the reforms enacted by Deng Xiaoping in 1990, there's been no looking back. If you get a chance to experience the Long Bar, try to get a table close to the window. It is the power table. Back in the day, when the ships rolled into the harbor, Shanghai's merchant elite would gather at the bar (aptly named for the large single piece of mahogany) to count their floating profits. The richest merchants would sit closest to the windows and the less polished, further inside. It was at the Long Bar that I was able to garner most of my insights into what is happening in China today. More on that in a moment.

The city is a world-class metropolis with massive, efficient infrastructure, two huge airports, a major rail hub for high-speed rail, and it also boasts the fastest train in the world. It's a Maglev train, capable of reaching speeds of 500 kilometers per hour—over 300 miles per hour. The train is a bit of an anomaly since it only runs on a short dedicated rail to the Shanghai Pudong International Airport . . . but in order to ride it, you need to take a ride outside the city center—it's a novelty more than anything else. It's worth a ride, but as I noticed when I flew on the Concorde, the full impact of how fast you are actually traveling comes from a screen telling you how fast, not some bodily experience!

Shanghai is the financial capital of mainland China. It is also where you will find the money, big money. Mansions and apartments costing more than $10 million are not uncommon. That money has to come from somewhere and in Shanghai, more than any other Chinese city, the money is old and very well preserved.

Leaps and Bounds

On my visit to Shanghai in 2006, I met with executives at several Chinese companies. Their presentation skills were impressive, and

I decided that I would take some time and "paper trade" their shares. The results weren't that good. Only one out of the four companies that I met with made significant gains, the others languished. The universal pitch from all of the companies at the time was "we can't lose, there are 1.3 billion people here." Well, it's just not that easy. If it were, then India and China would be the dominant global economies. The China population plays just don't cut it. For one thing, the vast majority of Chinese are poor, very poor by Western standards. Their lot in life has gotten better, but the incessant inflation in China has eaten away at much of the gains for the poor. They still toil away on small farms or big factories, making little money and certainly not shopping at Shanghai Tang. For all the money that seemingly flows into China, the margins are very low—it's about volume. And to stay competitive with up-and-coming neighbors like Vietnam, China has to keep prices low in the face of increasing costs for raw materials. It does this by exploiting its single largest asset: the workers.

In 2006 there was no talk or mention of labor unrest or social strife. Fast-forward to today and there are mini riots in some cities by workers complaining about both conditions and pay. There are no discounts if you're poor. Some countries, like India, operate a two-tiered pricing system, one price for the locals and one for foreigners. Subsidies are the order of the day. Not as much in China. The price for a gallon of gasoline is the same as in the United States, maybe a little higher. Yet, it costs less than 30 percent of what it would cost to take a taxi the same distance as in New York; the difference is the cost of labor. There is no discount for locals to enter the Forbidden City or the Great Wall or even if they want to buy a bottle of water while viewing the Terra Cotta Warriors in Xian. Now, on my most recent trip in 2011, I found prices to be higher than before, much higher. I am not rich, but I am not poor, either. And if I noticed such things, then there is no doubt that the locals are being pushed to the edge. There is a two-tiered system for wealth, however, in China. Either you have it or you don't. And, in Shanghai, if you have it, you flaunt it, much to the chagrin of the party officials in Beijing.

In Beijing, Volkswagens and Audis were the norm. In Shanghai, it's Mercedes Benz, Porsche, Range Rover, and Rolls Royce that rule the roads. Even a Ferrari or two makes an appearance every once in awhile. In Beijing, it's who you know . . . in Shanghai it's who you are. Some of my contacts that are well connected to the party intimated to me that the government is beginning to realize that the gap between rich and poor is not good for its image. China may be embarking on a capitalist agenda in public, but in private it is still the People's Republic and Communism is not quite dead. It cannot die just yet, not with the possibility of 1 billion angry workers who are seeing unimaginable wealth created, yet not participating in the fruits of what they consider their labor. The party is now sending out not-so-subtle messages to the wealthy to tone down their ostentatious public behavior and their over-the-top displays of wealth. It's just not good for business. China is not a meritocracy; it's a work in progress.

Party Time

The Shanghai elite knows how to party. My host on my 2011 visit was a high-level non-Chinese government official. I stayed at his residence and met with some great people in his business, government, and social network. For the sake of privacy I am not going to reveal any names—again, this is China that I'm talking about, and the last thing I want to do is to cause negative repercussions for individuals who provide me with great information and insight. And, in reality, revealing their names would not enhance the quality of the information I am providing to you.

Just before coming to the Long Bar on a rainy Friday evening, we had some drinks and appetizers at the new Portman Ritz-Carlton. It wasn't cheap. A few drinks and appetizers at the Flair Bar, located on the 58th floor, set me back over $400, making New York's Peninsula Hotel look like a bargain. I should have known when I walked into the private elevator, which was itself unique. Its walls were made from the bottoms of black wine bottles, which made it appear you were entering a cellar. The views from the balcony of the Flair Bar are some of the best in Shanghai—you can almost touch the Oriental Pearl Tower, the most recognizable of Shanghai's skyscrapers with its bulbous onion-shaped dome near the top.

Seated in a circle around the power table at the Long Bar, we began our evening's banter. My goal was to pin down some of the people and ask them questions that I knew would make them feel uncomfortable. But, I wanted real answers and not official fluff. I figured the time would be right after the third round of drinks.

The group consisted of three officials from foreign consulates, a real estate investor, the CEO of a public technology company, and a movie star. It made for interesting nonbusiness conversation, as well.

I had some issues I needed to clear up. The first was the perception that I had about China's overheated real estate market. The second was about the lack of trust and faith I have in the transparency of Chinese companies, especially those that are traded publicly. No pun intended, but there are red flags everywhere when analyzing Chinese companies. Source information is hard to come by. Auditors can be bought and sold. Accounting measures mean nothing, as the veracity of input information is suspect. And, documented corruption and graft by the Chinese government itself makes one pause.

In a web posting on the People's Bank of China site in June 2011—at the time of my visit—the Central Bank revealed that over the past 15 years, corrupt Chinese officials and employees of state-owned companies had absconded with more than $123 billion in cash, much of it finding its way to Europe, North America, Hong Kong, and Macau, sometimes simply stuffed in suitcases. And this is just the incidents that are documented. The posting was not on the site for very long, and the bank was quick to note that it had been posted by mistake. Just a few weeks later, Moody's Investment Service came out with a scathing report about accounting and informational inadequacy at 61 companies it analyzed, causing a one-day downdraft on the Hong Kong stock exchange. What worries me is not what we know exists, but how much we don't know—and that is almost always a heck of a lot worse.

Real Estate in China

Chinese real estate can be expensive, very expensive. One might think that there are few people who can afford to pay upward of $1,000 per square foot for real estate in what was not much more than a third-world country just two decades ago. One would be mistaken. In some places in Shanghai, Beijing, and other major cities in China, $1,000 per square foot would be a bargain. Paying $1 million in cash for an apartment in Shanghai is not a rarity. There are 125,000 millionaires in Shanghai alone!

Commercial real estate is even pricier. It seems unfathomable considering the number of skyscrapers that make up the skyline of Shanghai and Pudong, just across the river. But, let me tell you, the Shanghai skyline is as impressive as that of Manhattan in beauty and in scope. That said, I often wondered if there was really anyone in those buildings. I put the question to my real estate expert. He has major landholdings in Shanghai, both commercial and residential, and even a golf course operation. His answers surprised me. On commercial real estate his answers made sense. There is less of a bubble than many think. The reasoning behind it goes back to the attitudes of the Chinese vis-à-vis their western counterparts. For the longest time the Chinese have plied their trade with a lack of concern about where they were plying from. Dingy buildings in trash-strewn neighborhoods were the norm for corporate headquarters. When meeting with westerners they would do it off property or at a hotel. Things have changed. A result of pride and more money has made the Chinese rethink their digs. Now, companies locate themselves and their top-level employees in grade A office space across the hall from their Western counterparts. This, in addition to the thousands of non-Chinese companies and non-Chinese government entities that must make Shanghai their China headquarters, accounts for much of the demand and consumption of the office space inventory. Judging by the massive increases in activity in and around Shanghai and China in general that I have witnessed over the almost two decades I have been traveling to the country, I am inclined to give my real estate friend the benefit of the doubt regarding his explanation.

On residential property he had a different take. His belief is that property prices and inventory are both too high, especially in Shanghai and its environs. And, he is liquidating some of his holdings for the first time in more than 30 years as a real estate investor and owner. Part of it is because of the bubble caused by new money trying to find a home. Until recent laws were enacted to cool the market, such as a 50 percent down payment, limitations on the number of properties one can own, and proscribed legal occupancy periods before one can sell, it was not unusual for investors to put in bids for multiple properties. They did this with an amazing lack of risk because in many cases they needed nothing more that an indication of interest that they wanted to buy a property—no money for a deposit. They would then decide if they wanted to consummate the deal. They always did, which is why the system worked. But that is also because property prices continued to move higher by the month. Talk about good faith! If Chinese property values crash—and they have already slowed down—this good faith method of speculation will be entirely to blame.

We've Got Bad Accounting? You've Got WorldCom!

My discussions with the CEO of the public company were not as polite. Apparently neither one of us had drunk enough and the discussion was quite serious. I brought up my experiences with Chinese companies, the frequent use of public shell companies on the NASDAQ and Pink Sheets, accounting issues, corruption, and a general lack of transparency. He brought up WorldCom, Enron, Global Crossing, Bre-X, and Arthur Andersen.

Granted, we have had our share of fraud in the West. Definitely to a much bigger extent when measured in dollars. But, for the most part, we are comfortable with the transparency in U.S. companies and the accounting and auditing systems we have in place. The same cannot be said for Chinese companies. If it could be said for them, then the Chinese market would be the best-performing market in the world, not amongst the worst. Reality bites!

We talked about the accounting principles and he agreed that GAAP accounting was going to have to be observed by Chinese companies in toto at some point. His advice for investing in Chinese companies was actually quite simple. Invest in companies that are listed in Hong Kong (we're not talking about the big red chip companies) because they do have to meet strict requirements as compared to a lot of the crap that ends up listing on U.S. exchanges. His reasoning was that it was actually easier for the junk companies to list on U.S. exchanges because they would be too closely scrutinized in Hong Kong. In the United States the investment banks can get away with using a lot of boiler plate risk factors to cover their asses and then collect the fees that these suspect companies are more than happy to pay. If you want to invest in Chinese companies, invest in the ones that are owned by the State—they always make money!

More than 10,000 corrupt Chinese officials collectively took $120 billion out of the country in a 15-year spree of embezzlement, bribes, and defections, with some of the money ending up in Australia.

The revelations, laid bare in a report by the People's Bank of China that was never intended to be released to the public, shine an embarrassing spotlight on Chinese corruption, a problem seen by some as an Achilles' heel for the world's second-largest economy.

The report appears to have been mistakenly uploaded to an official website after winning a prize for the quality of its research.

Official corruption remains a source of disgust and frustration for the Chinese population at large.

The pervasiveness of money laundering outlined in the report offers a damning indictment of the government's wars on corruption in the run-up to the Communist Party's 90th anniversary on July 1.

A handful of prominent cases, including one that involved the Ministry of Railways, have rattled China since the beginning of the year, but just as destabilizing is the constant, low-level corruption that blights the lives of ordinary Chinese.

This week, at least eight new websites came online to offer increasingly infuriated Chinese the chance to vent their anger—on issues from gifts to doctors to encourage them to perform operations correctly to the rigging of trials.

The same angry online communities, riled by the palpably widening gulf between rich and poor, pushed last month for the death penalty to be given to Xu Maiyong, the former vice-mayor of Hangzhou, who was convicted of taking more than $30 million in bribes and embezzlement.

The research, whose revelations of corruption are breathtaking even by Chinese standards, estimates that between 16,000 and 18,000 officials may have fled the country with monumental hoards of ill-gotten money between the mid-1990s and 2008.

In one paragraph, the report, which had the words "internal data, store carefully" on the front page, cautioned that unchecked corruption was putting Communist rule at risk. "It is a direct threat to

(Continued)

(Continued)

the clean political structure of the Communist Party and harms the foundations of its power," it said.

Large amounts of the money, along with the officials who amassed it, headed for Australia or the United States.

Hong Kong was highlighted as a favorite springboard from which more senior officials could first leave mainland China and then flee to Commonwealth countries.

The defectors, according to the report, exploited both Hong Kong's status as an international aviation hub and the historic privilege of allowing residents to apply for visas on arrival in Commonwealth countries.

Less ambitious escapees, usually lower ranking malfeasants, made for Southeast Asian countries such as Burma and Thailand, while the more senior bribe-takers would head for tax havens in the Cayman Islands and Bermuda.

The most elite officials, said the report, would aim for Western countries such as Canada and the Netherlands, possibly moving through a small African or Eastern European country while documents were forged and time elapsed after their escape.

Some, revealed the People's Bank of China's 67-page report, smuggled money to the former Portuguese colony of Macau where it emerged, laundered through an accommodating casino, ready to fund a defector's life of opulence in Russia or Mongolia. The trail of officials bearing bags of banknotes and crossing from Shenzhen was described in the report as being "like ants moving houses."

The report, which was compiled by the central bank's money-laundering analysts and called "The Routes That Our Country's Corrupt Officials Transfer Assets Abroad," described eight main conduits for moving money out of China.

Methods ranged from the high-risk option of a suitcase full of cash and a dash to the border to convoluted networks of foreign intermediaries.

Senior managers from listed companies or state-owned enterprises, it said, would disguise the illegal transfers beneath legitimate remittances, cloaking the process with forged contracts and other documents that were destroyed.

The three-year-old document appears to have made it, fleetingly, into the public domain this week because the research was deemed so good.

The report won first place in the China Society for Finance and Banking's annual awards for financial research and, despite the warnings that it was for internal central bank consumption only, was put online as the winner of the prize.

It was removed from the People's Bank website moments after domestic media spotted it and began publishing its findings.

Leo Lewis, *The Australian*, June 17, 2011, www.theaustralian.com.au/news/world/accidentally-released-report-reveals-embarrassing-extent-of-chinese-corruption/story-e6frg6so-1226076938605.

Places

The Ritz Carlton Shanghai, 1376, Nanjing Xi Lu, Shanghai 200040 China, Phone: (86 21) 6279 8888 Fax: (86 21) 6279 8800. The Long Bar, The Waldorf Astoria, Shanghai www.waldorfastoriashanghai.com/english/maps_directions

Nightclubs of Note

Prive

Housed above the Dolce and Gabbana Bar on the Bund

6号 Zhongshan East 1st Road, Huangpu, Shanghai, China

(86 21) 3331 7585

The M1nt

www.m1ntglobal.com/club-shanghai

Investing in China

China is less of an emerging market than many others. Many argue whether it should even be categorized in the same company as countries like Cambodia, Thailand, or Chile. I would agree. Instead, it's probably better to categorize emerging markets as tiers. I like to use a three-tiered system for emerging markets.

Tier 1 countries are those that cannot turn back the clock and become real emerging markets. This means that they have the financial wherewithal to defend their markets and populations against a major shock, the kind that Mexico has faced numerous times in the past half century. They can, in effect bail themselves out because they are not so indebted that their economies would fail without the intervention of outside countries.

Tier 2 countries are those that have made the jump from subsistence economies to functioning economies based on trade and commerce. They are not reliant on aid from the outside world just to keep afloat. Aid for commercial enterprise is different. These countries are still subject to shocks that will damage their markets, their economies, and possibly their social frameworks, as well. A good example is a country like Vietnam.

Tier 3 countries are basically the youngest emerging markets. These are markets with no real way of participating in global commerce without massive amounts of foreign aid. They have no real markets to speak of in terms of a stock exchange, and wealth creation is still in its infancy. These countries can tip back into the abyss of economic oblivion at the drop of a hat . . . and often do. Examples of countries that would fit into this tier would be Uganda or New Guinea or Nicaragua.

The Top of the First Tier

China is at the top of the ladder of first tier emerging markets. The only reason that it does not make it out of emerging markets status, despite its massive wealth, is that China is not a transparent economy and is still a country that is ruled by a single party without democratic aspirations. It also has a bad habit of cracking down violently on dissent and does not respect freedom of information.

China does offer several attractive reasons for investors to consider it, however. It is the world's fastest growing major economy. That presents opportunities. It does have functioning stock markets in Shanghai and Hong Kong. It needs to continue to grow in order to provide opportunity for its massive population, which is making a transition from third world to first world. This transition and the potential for social upset if it fails, is the driving force behind China's relentless growth policy.

The best way to present China is to use a SWOT analysis, followed by specific recommendations. SWOT refers to strengths, weaknesses, opportunities, and threats. The recommendations that I will make will not be in specific companies. In my experience it is very hard for investors to make money in emerging markets with recommendations that are more than a few weeks or months old. These markets are by nature dynamic and most, if not all, companies lack transparency or track records that would make me comfortable in recommending them. Instead, emerging markets must be treated as trading vehicles until they finally leave the emerging designation behind and emerge. Singapore is a good example of such a country.

Strengths

Money. China sits on over $3 trillion of reserves. It has more cash on hand than the annual GDP of most of the countries in the world combined. It boasts a large population base of fairly well-educated workers. China has over 300 million people that make up its middle class. These are educated individuals who are hard-working and ambitious. They are the backbone of China's emergence from an export driven economy to one that will be self-sustaining.

A one-party system. This allows China to forge ahead with infrastructure development without regard to dissent. For a country the size of China to grow as fast as it can and raise the living standards of all of its people in a span of just 20 years, the one-party system was and is invaluable.

History of capitalism and success. There have been few major empires since the Romans. China, Russia, India, Great Britain, France, Spain, Austria/Germany, and the United States are the major ones. China was at one time the wealthiest country on the face of the earth. It has history. It all came to a crashing halt in the latter part of the nineteenth and twentieth centuries, but the history is not lost on the Chinese. They have a chip on their collective shoulders and to them it's not a matter of "if" but "when" they once again regain their place of prosperity.

Markets. China has a well-oiled mechanism of public markets for commerce to take place. While Shanghai is the place that China wants as its global financial capital, in truth, Hong Kong is the more respected market from the point of view of the rest of the world. It's rare, indeed, for a country to have two major financial centers and rarer still to have one country with two sepa-rate currencies, as well. Hong Kong has a reputation as a respected exchange; Shanghai does not. This is the result of the stronger regulations and established practices left behind by the British. Hong Kong still maintains a type of independence in certain mat-ters from the mainland that allows it to be more part of the global brotherhood of markets. But make no mistake. While China agreed to allow Hong Kong to operate in an independent fashion for at least 50 years after the handover from the British, it is still Beijing that calls the shots. Under a "one country, two systems" environ-ment, Hong Kong is allowed to maintain a capitalist system . . . as long as it does not create waves. The population of Hong Kong is quite fiercely independent and demonstrations are not unusual. However, I am certain that any serious affront to the powers in Beijing would be dealt with quickly and painfully.

The Hong Kong stock exchange is an outlet for Chinese com-panies that want to list on a more respectable exchange. It is also an exchange where foreigners can readily and easily trade shares of both mainland companies and Hong Kong-based companies.

Clout. As one of the world's biggest consumers of resources—and on its way to becoming the single largest—China commands a lot of attention from producers. It imports massive amounts of raw materials daily to fuel its growth, and that gives the country a huge voice in the global community and the power to affect global pric-ing of commodities. In the past decade China has also embarked on a buying and investing binge, making major investments in raw material-producing nations, especially in cash-starved regions of the world like Africa and, closer to home, Mongolia.

Weaknesses

China is a political and social time bomb. As it gets richer and as its population becomes more educated, it risks more civil disobe-dience. For now, the government has been able to crack down on dissidence through the use of technology to restrict access to infor-mation that could be damaging to its reputation internally. For the most part the Han Chinese, the majority, are happy with the wealth creation and social mobility the country has experienced for two decades. However, the incidences of revolt against government restrictions on freedom of speech are rising. The main reason for this is the perception amongst the population that the government is corrupt, especially at local levels. Wealth is being distributed unevenly and, while in a meritocracy like the United States that has not been much of an issue, in a place like China where class warfare has not been the norm, it is fast becoming an issue.

Ethnic strife is also an issue. China's population is diverse. The country is huge and in the outer provinces ethnic minorities are pressing for freedoms of religion and self-governance. Incidents of terrorism, rioting, and general public disturbances are growing, as these provinces have not bought into the homogeneity that Beijing is selling. And, because the majority of the wealth and commerce is being conducted by and between the ethnic Han Chinese majority, not everyone is seeing their fortunes rise. In fact, the Han are now moving westward into the less "Chinese" provinces and trying to homogenize them. Tibet is a good example. It is swarming with Han Chinese now that China has pushed for a policy to bring Tibet into China. Ethnic groups like the Uighurs consider themselves completely separate and distinct from the Chinese in every respect—from religion to race. China has been cracking down on this so-called autonomous region located in the southwest part of the country. A lack of understanding and tolerance by the Chinese of the non-Han groups presents a major stumbling block for China's ascent to first-world status.

Opportunities

China has more opportunities for wealth creation than any other place on earth. Most of this is by virtue of the massive population that is now mobilized to move upward economically. Now, those opportunities are largely internal and there have been very few Western companies that have been either successful or allowed to take part in this growth. For the most part, the Western companies that have made money from China are those in the resource sector that have been selling everything to the Chinese from wheat to copper to fast food chains!

This means there are a lot of companies in China, companies that you can invest in that can make money from the growth that is yet to come. As individuals, the Chinese are well behind the

developed world in per capita income. According to the World
Bank, China's per capita income is around $7,500, which puts
it behind Ecuador and about 94th on the list. Average per capita
income worldwide is around $10,000. The United States is seventh
at about $48,000. Interestingly, Hong Kong would be eighth if not
tied to China, with around $45,000 per capita. But, on a country-
to-country rank, China has surpassed all countries except for the
United States and is second on the list. For per capita GDP, China
ranks 94th again at around $4,500 compared to $47,000 for the
United States. Therein lies the opportunity. China has massive
amounts of consumption per capita left to go. Unlike other countries that have stalled out, China is still growing its GDP at near
double-digit rates, and it has the economic and monetary muscle to
continue. This makes the consumer sector a massive profit opportunity as the people in China are only now beginning to discover
the luxuries that the West has enjoyed for decades—not necessities,
but luxuries, like dishwashers!

Threats

China faces more internal threats than external. As a communist
country it has to balance a fine line between freedom and control.
Social unrest is the single greatest threat that can pull China into
chaos. It has no choice but to keep the pedal on the gas to keep
growing and assimilating its massive rural population into an urban
population. The vast majority of the people, as they get educated,
will clamor for more and a more even distribution of wealth—
China is not a democracy that was weaned on wealth based on
work, but rather on wealth based on the common good.

Ethnic tensions could spill over and cause serious, violent
confrontations, which could damage China's global image. As
the world's factory and largest exporter, China cannot afford a
boycott.

China faces interesting times trying to convince the world
that Taiwan and Tibet want to be part of its hegemony willingly.
Tensions continue to be high at times and, as recently as July 2011,
China expressed massive displeasure at the United States president
for meeting with the Dalai Lama, the spiritual leader of Tibetan
Buddhists.

Growth

China must grow to succeed. This means massive inflationary pressures will continue as it sucks up raw materials. Per capita oil consumption by the Chinese is a fraction of that in the United States. Yet, the Chinese are driving more, electrifying more, and consuming more. This has resulted in an increased average price per barrel of oil for almost a decade, and that trend is not going to reverse until alternate fuels are used.

Pollution

Much of China's water supply is tainted. It is the world's biggest factory and most days in the major cities you are unable to see more than a few hundred yards. The haze seems almost permanent. China faces major health concerns that are the result of people living longer but ingesting more pollutants. Chinese companies are routinely found to use harmful chemicals in the production of everything from consumer goods to baby formula.

Possibly the greatest threat China faces is itself. As a major force in the world and in the region that it occupies, China can have a massive impact on global events. The country's stature is growing daily, but it has yet to declare its intentions. At times, the country looks to be a strong part of the international community such as when it hosts the Olympics, for example. At other times it sides with known despotic nations like Iran or threatens military force against Taiwan. China is growing economically and politically, but it is not allowing itself to grow socially. The one-party system still dictates everything from shaping views on global warming to blocking e-mails of individuals it considers a threat. China is a wild card that has the power to become a first-world superpower economically, militarily, and socially, but it has to let go of its authoritarian bent first.

CHAPTER 2

India

HEAVEN OR HELL?

I ask myself that question each time I visit India. Another former empire nation, India is likely the country with the most potential of any Tier 2 emerging market—if only it could get its act together.

My first visit to the country was in 1997. After stopping in Hong Kong for the handover, I boarded a flight for New Delhi. As I recall, it was one of the scariest flights I have ever been on (besides the Singapore Airlines flight I was on leaving Taipei when I witnessed one of the four engines exploding from the upper deck). The combination of unstable air from the monsoon and the mountain ranges made for a turbulent flight with a spectacular lightning show.

Landing at the airport in Delhi was an interesting experience. Besides the fact that I am the first member of my family in three generations to set foot in the country of my origin, India assaults you the minute you land. Normally, when a plane lands, the vents are opened to let in fresh air from the outside. When landing in India, I would recommend that the pilot *not* open the vents. The pollution is so bad that all I could do was clutch my throat and reach for a bottle of water in my backpack. Yes, it's that bad. On my last trip, just a couple of years ago, that part had not changed. I have been to India several times in the past 15 years and the pollution is getting worse each time. That's not a good sign. I would have to rank it ahead of China in this respect, not a position that the country should be proud of. But, as in almost all emerging markets, there is a high price to pay for progress, and the argument against pollution is not met with friendly ears.

The second thing you notice about Delhi's airport is that it's pretty much a dump, like most airports in India that I have had the pleasure of visiting. It was built in the 1970s and looks as if it was painted for a second time in the late 1970s. I'm sure many of the offices still have shag carpeting—the lounges are a joke. A new terminal opened recently—I'm sure it is an improvement.

This is pretty much the case throughout India. It just doesn't seem to want to move as fast into the twenty-first century as does China. If someone even utters India and China in the same sentence when it comes to growth or any other comparison, they are either lacking in scruples or have never visited both countries. There is no comparison; hence China is a Tier 1 country and India is not. Now, this has absolutely no bearing on the opportunity to make money. In that regard, India may actually be a better long-term bet.

The airport is crowded with very little in the way of order anywhere. There is a lot of security, thin men in berets carrying sub machine guns. It's a no-smoking terminal, but somehow the whiff of tobacco smoke is omnipresent as are the butts in the corners of the hallways. Once you clear security and head outside, it is different . . . well, at least different from my first visit. Invariably all flights coming into Delhi arrive at 2 A.M. or 4 A.M. It's really ridiculous to expect anyone to navigate that early. Fortunately, unlike China, everyone here speaks English, some better than folks at home!

On my first visit, I really could not tell where the airport ended and where the street began. Beggars were everywhere, hawkers trying to arrange taxis, random people just staring at you as if you had landed from another planet. It was a zoo. Now, however, there is a little more civility. The madding crowd is no longer congregating at the steps of the airport and that makes exiting a lot easier. Although, I do secretly miss the noisy throng that is representative of the country in general.

Progress

Leaving the airport, I expected a leisurely ride to the Oberoi with Dr. Zakir Hussain Marg. It was anything but. I could not keep from looking out of the windows, at least not in 1997. There were people sleeping on the sidewalks, not in a temporary fashion but in what seemed like bunks, three high. It was a disturbing sight, but they seemed to be quite content. It was a sight I would see over and over again in this country where a person's lot in life is seemingly graciously accepted. On my last trip, the sidewalks were less occupied to the point of actually being quite empty.

The Oberoi is beautiful—once you get past actually seeing haze in the lobby and the smell of freshly sprayed insecticide. It's clad in marble with the feel of a five-star facility. A huge pool is located just below the lobby and the hotel sits in a very large compound. A word of warning. In India there are only two classes of hotels, five-star and everything else. If there is one thing that you should not think twice about, it is spending the money on a good hotel, preferably one that has grounds. After a hot day in the dirty, crowded, noisy streets, one needs an escape. When choosing hotels to stay at, you will rarely go wrong staying at either an Oberoi-branded hotel or a Taj-branded hotel.

One thing that you will notice right away is that Indians don't all look the way you expect them to. They're not all short, or dark, or smiling. At least that seems to be the way they're generally portrayed in the West. What you will find is a melting pot like few other places. You will see tall, slender, fair-skinned girls like the desk clerks at the Oberoi, or you may see someone from Kashmir with sand brown hair and green eyes, or a tall Punjabi or sikh, or someone who is short and dark. You have to remember that India has been invaded an untold number of times by people with ancestries that range from Europe to the steppes of Asia. The variation in the peoples of this country is truly a sight to see.

The Oberoi, New Delhi
Dr. Zakir Hussain Marg
New Delhi - 110003, India
Telephone : +91 11 2436 3030
Facsimile : +91 11 2436 0484
Updated July 8, 2010

The first day is always disorienting. I recall once opening the dark wooden shutters of my very well-appointed hotel room to see what I thought was a silhouette of the moon, only to realize that I was looking at the faint outline of the sun behind a thick layer of haze. The food in India is wonderful, and I recommend a hearty breakfast at the hotel each day. Every possible food is available and the service has never been anything short of outstanding.

New Delhi

Delhi, pronounced Dilli, is a city that has been destroyed and built over many times. It has been the capital of India many different times as well, usually at the whim of the Moghul emperor in power at the time. Most recently, Delhi became the capital city of India under the British Raj who transferred the capital from Kolkota (Calcutta) in 1911. It officially became the capital in 1947, after India gained independence from the British. It is not the financial capital of India; that title belongs to Mumbai (Bombay), but it is the seat of power in the country and a very different place. It is much like Beijing in terms of seriousness compared with Shanghai in terms of fun.

Delhi has its share of awesome architecture ranging from the Qut'b Minar, a tall tower built in the 1200s to the Edwin Luytens architectural masterpieces that are the capital's governmental buildings. Delhi, like the rest of India, is teeming with life and home to some of the country's best universities, one of the reasons I made a visit here in the mid-2000s. My mission was to do some groundwork with a couple of my colleagues regarding opening up an office in India, or at the least hiring some of the homegrown talent we had heard so much about.

My visits to the various universities astounded me. Many were not pretty on the outside, housed as they were in crumbling buildings. Inside it was little different—think old-American-schoolhouse-on-the-prairie type furniture. Some of the technical colleges were housed in more modern facilities. But, in India, looks are deceiving. The real treasures here are the students. They are smart, hard-working, ambitious . . . and cheap.

I met with several placement officials at the universities and what I learned amazed me. The norm was for a graduate, with a graduate degree, to be hired by one of the large IT companies. Many would provide training and housing in addition to a job. The top companies would offer a package worth about $18,000 to $25,000 for a top-level student with an advanced degree. The same person would command close to six figures in the United States. That is why western companies have such big operations in India and why companies like Infosys are so successful. I arrived at the end of the school year and all of the graduates had already been placed. Now, think about that. If the top-ranked graduate students are only pulling down $18,000, think of how little it cost to hire four-year grads from the best schools. This is why the future of places like India and China is so bright. They have a seemingly unlimited supply of extremely well educated, ambitious talent who would jump through hoops for a job twice as hard as one they could find in the United States, for 10 to 20 percent of the money. It's not hard to figure out who's going to win this economic battle in the end.

The Short Tour

Personally, I would not recommend spending more than a couple of days in Delhi. Unless you're up for some serious sightseeing, there are many more exciting places to visit in India. Delhi does have something, though, that is not found anywhere else in India: the Chandni Chowk. Entering this age-old market is an adventure in itself. Think of the worst driving and traffic you've ever seen and multiply it ten-fold. It is nothing short of a great buzz navigating your way through the crowds whether in your car or on foot or in a tuk-tuk. On the bumper of every vehicle there is a sticker that reads "Please Honk" and they mean it!

Entering the Chandni Chowk you drive past a street full of barbers cutting hair and shaving men's beards on the sidewalk. Not just one or two, dozens. In front of you at all times are little kids doing acrobatics and begging for a handout. Once you enter one of the main streets of the market your senses are assaulted by the smells of spices, cooking, and, of course, the body odor. Every square inch of the streets are occupied either by vendors, beggars, street urchins, or buyers. Walk around one corner and you'll see a cow being fed by its owner. Around another is a beautiful wedding procession, colorful, loud, and jolly. Around another is a Sufi mosque, and around the next is the flower market with garlands as far as the eye can see. Commerce in India is a way of life and the Chandni Chowk has been in existence on this very spot for centuries. It is a sight not to be missed. Of course, the pickpockets know this as well—beware. There is little violent crime in a place like Delhi, but petty theft is pervasive.

The Jama Masjid is another one of Delhi's great sights. A beautiful mosque that was commissioned by Shah Jehan, the Moghul Emperor who built the Taj Mahal, it is open to visitors daily. You'll notice that the predominant form of architecture in Delhi (of really historic buildings) is of Moghul heritage. It was the Moghuls who arguably brought India out of its dark ages and also caused its collapse. They left behind scores of fantastic buildings and complexes, like Fatehpur Sikri, made of red sandstone, and the Taj Mahal in Agra. There is no lack of outstanding architecture in India, both Hindu and Muslim, and much of it is fantastically preserved. There is no love lost between Hindus and Muslims and in much of Indian society, while members of the two religions coexist, there is a noticeable social and business chasm between them that I encountered in my dealings with both groups.

My favorite part about Delhi is leaving it. India has much more to offer than a polluted, noisy capital city. It has its charms and Delhi-ites love it like no other place, but it's not the best introduction to the country. If you must, the best time to visit is between November and March when the weather is cooler—and it can get cold. I've been there in the monsoon season, and that is a time to avoid at all costs, unless 100-degree, wet, humid days are what you are seeking. Delhi is also a great staging point for a visit to Katmandu and Mt. Everest, only a short hour-and-a-half flight to the north. I won't be talking about Nepal, but if you go, stay at the Yak and Yeti in Katmandu, a beautiful hotel in a city and country that is one of my favorites to visit for recreation.

Mum-BUY

There are few places that I have visited in my travels that are as vibrant as Mumbai. Formerly Bombay (from the Portuguese *bom baim* or "good little bay"), this coastal city on India's West Coast is the country's financial and entertainment capital. Choked with traffic day and night, the city manages to function in grand style. From beautiful Victorian-era buildings such as the main train station and post office, to skyscrapers in the financial district and mansions in the Malabar Hill area, Mumbai offers a glimpse of cosmopolitan India. Bollywood, India's prolific entertainment business, calls Mumbai home, and if you are looking for glitz and glamour, you'll find it here.

Mumbai is also home to the Bombay Stock Exchange (BSE). It's an interesting place. The exchange building is kind of modern—it's tall, has lots of glass, and looks like it could pass for a mini skyscraper in any modern city. Unfortunately it is surrounded by fairly ugly buildings and is on a street that would easily pass for a poor street in Manhattan. Inside, the exchange floor is beautiful. Air-conditioning is still a little spotty, though, and it can get quite warm in the summer. On my first visit here I met with the head of the stock exchange who was still sweating despite the window unit in his office.

It was an interesting time, my first visit. The Asian financial crisis was just beginning and India was in the midst of a bull run. It weathered the storm quite well, in hindsight. India is less prone to be affected by external crises than many other countries. Its currency is not convertible, its population tends to buy locally made goods, and it's still largely an agrarian economy. The low level of reliance on imported and exported goods makes it less likely to be affected during global downturns. Frankly, the situation is not by choice; India has been a relatively poor country for decades. Things are changing now, but not for the majority of the population. Like China, when you have more than a billion people, even a minority of the population is bigger than the entire population of the United States.

The BSE has been on a tear over the past decade increasing in value ten fold since 2001 and holding those gains today. The financial crisis affected the BSE, but it bounced back with a vengeance. See Table 2.1.

In terms of historical valuation the market is trading close to the higher end of its historical averages. It hasn't reached the absurd levels it reached in the mid-90s when the price earnings ratio reached 45 and price to book was 6.5. There are three explanations for India's strong market performance. First, the market is extremely small in terms of capitalization at $1.6 trillion. Sounds like a big number, but that market cap is less than that of the five largest U.S. companies. Second, the Indian market is still the recipient of strong Foreign Direct Inflows, which can goose prices in a small market. Finally, Indian stocks are trading well because there

Table 2.1   Bombay Stock Exchange 2001 to 2011

Year	Open	High	Low	Close	Price/ Earnings	Price/ Book Value	Dividend Yield
2001	3,990.65	4,462.11	2,594.87	3,262.33	17.60	2.51	1.83
2002	3,262.01	3,758.27	2,828.48	3,377.28	15.22	2.30	2.14
2003	3,383.85	5,920.76	2,904.44	5,838.96	15.02	2.49	2.14
2004	5,872.48	6,617.15	4,227.50	6,602.69	17.26	3.28	2.01
2005	6,626.49	9,442.98	6,069.33	9,397.93	16.21	3.94	1.58
2006	9,422.49	14,035.30	8,799.01	13,786.91	20.18	4.75	1.35
2007	13,827.77	20,498.11	12,316.10	20,286.99	22.25	5.32	1.10
2008	20,325.27	21,206.77	7,697.39	9,647.31	18.22	4.20	1.29
2009	9,720.55	17,530.94	8,047.17	17,464.81	18.08	3.42	1.43
2010	17,473.45	21,108.64	15,651.99	20,509.09	21.71	3.67	1.12
2011	20,621.61	20,664.80	17,295.62	18,502.38	20.19	3.51	1.16

is underlying growth in the economy. It's a good situation for now. But India, like every other emerging market, is prone to massive volatility and is not immune from market manipulation.

The Big Bull

When I first began covering emerging markets in 1992 as the research director for *Taipan*, an emerging market publication, India was on my screen for all the wrong reasons. It was the subject of global scorn because of a massive market manipulation pulled off by the infamous Harshad Mehta (infamous there), more fondly referred to as the Big Bull.

The Big Bull was very bullish on Indian equities. After making his way up the exchange ladder from a small-time stock broker, Mehta developed a following based on his trading prowess. Little did anyone know that this prowess was the result of heavy market manipulation. Mehta would borrow money through an intricate scheme where his funds would be guaranteed by government paper during a 15-day float period. He would use the money to buy up shares of companies and, through his promotion of the upward momentum that seems to draw in buyers, he would make enough to pay back the funds from margin. This continued for a period of months during which he likely caused a huge bull market in Indian share . . . until he, and ultimately the market, crashed, as well.

The market has never seen manipulation of that scale since. But, it points out the weaknesses inherent in emerging markets. At the time, the BSE's market cap was less than $100 billion, and that makes for a very tight float considering that it had thousands of small-cap companies listed. Add to this the lax oversight by regulators and it's not surprising that it happened and can happen again in just about any market. It was no secret that the Indian exchange was nothing more than a fixed game. One prominent exchange official who I met on my first visit told me in not so many words that the market was rigged. It was several years before I had enough faith to recommend an Indian stock.

A Profitable Afternoon at the Cricket Club

In 2006, my colleagues Greg Grillot and James Boric and I met at the Cricket Club of India as guests of Ajit Dayal, a prominent and successful fund manager. Once a bastion of the city's elite, the Cricket Club has not changed much since its founding in 1933. The pitch is beautiful and still mowed and seeded by hand, as I witnessed during lunch. The food at the club is superb, especially the chicken tikka (moist morsels of chicken breast marinated in a mélange of delicious spices and then cooked in a tandoor oven made of clay at temperatures north of 900 degrees).

Ajit is a good friend of mine. He got his start as a lead manager of a $2 billion fund for Vanguard back in the '80s. Today, he's the founder and manager of Quantum Mutual Funds and is the quintessential value manager who has been making money for his clients in the Indian markets. You can read more about Ajit here: http://ajitdayal.com/ajit_bio.html.

As a fund manager, Ajit is very well connected. He and his team are in constant contact with executives at major and minor Indian companies, and they put out a lot of very good research—the type you don't see coming from Wall Street.

Our visit this time was actually to set up a future visit planned for the end of 2007 with a group of investors for a more in-depth, boots-on-the-ground investigation of the country and companies.

India is a very closed, insulated country. Much of the wealth is controlled by a minority of the population. A few families control much of the major industry—Tata, Ambani, Mittal, Godrej, and Premji—are but a few family names that dot the list of wealthiest people on the planet. These are the Carnegies, the Rockefellers, and the Gateses of India controlling stakes in industrials, energy, and technology companies.

One of the most fascinating clans in India is the Parsis. The Parsis have an interesting story, and their foresight and ability to create wealth is one of the major reasons that India is where it is today. They are universally respected for their business acumen. If India is a closed community, then the Parsis are the most impregnable part of the community for reasons that may not be apparent on the surface. The most prominent of the Parsi families is Tata, owners of everything from luxury car groups like Range Rover and Jaguar to hotels and information technology. One of the largest private employers in India, they have business interests in more than 80 countries in the world. But, as Parsis, they are facing a unique situation in regards to succession. The Parsis are a dying clan as they do not intermarry and are not open to allowing others to join their religion.

They arrived in India in the 1200s from Persia (hence the name Parsi) in search of religious freedom and commerce. They are believers in Zoroastrianism. India, for all its faults, has been a country that has, with few exceptions, allowed the practice of just about any and every form of religion. There are fewer than 125,000 Parsis in the entire world and about 70,000 in India. Yet, many of their members rank as the wealthiest in India.

As the agenda took form, I began to get more excited about the companies that would be presenting to us. The one that excited me the most was ICICI Bank (NYSE:IBN), India's second largest bank. The bank is highly profitable, technologically advanced, and aggressively focused on the retail segment of the population with strong operations and growth directed to consumer lending needs like vehicles and housing, two of the fastest growing segments for loan growth in any emerging market.

The other company I was looking forward to visiting was Infosys (NASDAQ:INFY), the information technology giant that has dominated the global stage with its presence in the enterprise solution market. Basically it provides the technology and manpower to help companies use technology and systems to operate more efficiently and, hopefully, more profitably. Companies like Infosys and others like Wipro and Tata are strong players in IT globally. One of the key reasons is education and the strength of Indian universities when it comes to producing high-caliber graduates. The other reason is the Indian rupee.

India is a very inexpensive country on many measures. As in China, if you wanted to live on ground level, like the locals, you could probably do it on a few dollars per day. Food is cheap, housing is cheap, transportation is cheap . . . not that you would necessarily want to live like a local in either country. But, India differs a little from China in the respect that the government is quite fond of bestowing subsidies, and the population is quite fond of receiving them. That makes for an artificial pricing environment and one that has to change. India has a two-tiered pricing system for locals and foreigners. For example, I could be sitting next to an Indian national on a flight from Mumbai to Chennai. I would be paying $200, while he would be paying $50. The same is true with hotels. My room at the Taj Mahal Palace in Mumbai cost around $300 in high season, while his would be less than half that.

The Indian rupee is not a convertible currency. It does not trade on the world markets, and its value is strictly controlled by the Reserve Bank of India (RBI). The government likes to keep the rupee cheap. It keeps foreigners investing in India, buying its goods and services, and it keeps the tourism market healthy. Its artificially low rate also means that locals have to contend with high inflation on goods not subsidized by the government. Still, it's possible to have a four-course meal in a good Indian restaurant for less than $10. A better one will set you back around $20 . . . and if you're in Mumbai, you should make it a point to eat at Khyber near the Taj Mahal Palace.

Khyber
Kalaghoda, Fort
Mumbai, Maharashtra, India
022 22673228

A word to the wise—the food is both spicy and hot, so be sure to ask for it to be toned down a little.

Down to Business

Mumbai may be the financial heart of India, but the real growth has been taking place in places like Bangalore and Hyderabad. These southern cities are where the Indian tech giants and start-ups alike make their homes. One major reason so many Indian companies are very successful is their ability to attract very low priced talent. But, it goes a step further.

On my last trip, my colleague Chris Mayer, editor of *Capital & Crisis*, and I visited the campuses of Infosys and the infamous Satyam (in 2009, the company was found to have cooked its books for almost a decade and what was once a billion-dollar enterprise collapsed overnight into a penny stock, only to regain its footing under new management).

Both campuses were located off side roads that seemed quite normal by Indian standards, nothing to suggest the billion-dollar enterprises hidden in the woods. Now, this is no Silicon Valley by any means. Poverty is rife throughout the country and just being in Cyberabad (Hyderabad's nickname), does not provide immunity from day-to-day reality.

In Bangalore we met with several local officials before heading off to see the tech centers. They gave us a slide show explaining how the municipal government was working to improve the infrastructure. An hour later we were traveling on a pot-holed road fearing for our lives. This type of wishful thinking is not uncommon in India. The politicians say the right things but rarely deliver. The situation is starkly different once inside the campuses of these high-tech companies.

On the Infosys campus, we were driven around in golf carts through a sprawling, beautifully manicured property dotted with modern buildings, some of which are striking in their architecture—including a glass pyramid at the Bangalore campus. Tennis courts, soccer fields, food courts, and dorms are the norm. Infosys' campus in Mysore spans 337 acres of land—the largest "corporate university" in the world.

Landing a job at Infosys is like winning the lottery in India. Once accepted you are relocated to a campus, housed, trained, fed, and able to live a life of comparative luxury. In return the company expects you to perform to world standards. For the average Indian, even in the middle class, landing a position at Infosys is like being transported from India to California overnight. Loyalty is paramount and competition is keen even though the salary is one-fifth that of a similar position in the United States or Europe. Looking at it from a pure numbers perspective considering India's vast population, landing a top job at Infosys or the like is probably on par with making the NBA.

Our hosts lead us through a presentation at their media center explaining the dynamics of IT consulting and how seamless it is now that communication is so efficient. A roster of clients at Infosys includes major players like Verizon, ABB, Analog Devices, and so on. It's actually quite difficult to get a client roster for the company because many of its clients are not happy about releasing details of their relationship with Infosys. Backlash from citizens, especially in the United States, regarding outsourcing of jobs has made it a very touchy subject in many circles. Yet, at a time when the United States was in a recession following the financial crisis of 2008 and 2009 and in the period of slow growth in 2010 and 2011, Infosys shares hit record highs as more businesses naturally turned to the company to save costs. This is India's promise: a low-cost center of highly technical operations in a country where English is spoken everywhere and is most definitely the language of commerce. That was one of the issues I had with China; it's one of the few major world powers where you cannot operate comfortably or even visit without an interpreter.

Companies like Infosys, Wipro, and Tata dominate IT consultancy in India and, while priced for perfection today, they do suffer sharp drops when the Indian markets correct, which happens every two or three years. They are among the best bets for participating in the Indian markets. The key is to wait for a correction and then trade.

Infrastructure is likely the easiest "sure thing" play for India. Unlike China, which has spent over a trillion dollars on infrastructure projects in the past 20 years, India has spent a lot of time instead. Indian officials have spent time talking about the trillions needed to improve, build, and maintain their infrastructure. High-speed rail—it's not going to happen. It's hard enough to maintain the low-speed rail systems here. Airports? They're a throwback to the 1970s in almost every respect. Roads? It takes a good hour and a half to get from the airport in Mumbai to the Taj Mahal Palace at the Gateway of India on Apollo Bunder—a distance of about 20 miles from the airport. It is my favorite hotel in Mumbai, a world-class experience from the outstanding food and nightclubs to the well-appointed rooms and service. Be sure to stay in the historic wing. This is the same hotel that suffered a terrorist attack in November 2008. I was staying there just months before. The hotel has since reopened in all of its grandeur, and I would not hesitate to stay there again.

The ride from the airport to the hotel in Mumbai is an event in its own right and should tell you a thing or two about the road situation. As I mentioned, the ride during rush hour will take more than an hour—believe it. Picture this: We are in a large coach. Next to us is a taxicab. Next to the cab is a cart being pulled by a horse. Next to that is a tuk-tuk. Next to the tuk-tuk is a scooter. Next to the scooter is a private car. Next to the private car is a man on foot pulling a wooden trailer. Next to him is a cow. And running around these various forms of transport are pedestrians trying to get across the street—there are few traffic lights and scofflaws are the rule of the day. Oh, I forgot to mention, multiply the scene above by a few thousand and then put them all on a street that would qualify as a minor street in a U.S. city and you will get the drift. Yet, with all of this traffic and mayhem, I have yet to witness one accident on the streets. The local cabbies here (and in China and Vietnam and Thailand and I am sure many other places) have a saying: "good brakes, good horn, and good luck." The traffic situation in India is by far the worst I have witnessed in all of my travels. Yet, the country manages to thrive and prosper. It's a scene I like to call "controlled chaos." I can only imagine how much wealthier and more productive India could actually be if it actually did improve its infrastructure.

Larsen and Toubro or L&T is likely the best pure infrastructure play in India. An $11.7 billion company, it has more work that it can handle; its order book, or backlog, is currently more than three times its annual sales. Involved in everything from heavy engineering to energy, the company has seen revenue double in the past five years and quadruple in the past 10. The markets have taken note of this and its shares are amongst the best performers over the past decade. It's difficult to project where the share price will go in the short term, but over the longer term this is another company that you need to own if you want to bet on India's infrastructure growth. And if there is one certainty it is this: India will not grow without spending many hundreds of billions of dollars on its infrastructure. You can get more information on Larsen and Toubro at www.larsentoubro.com/lntcorporate/common/ui_templates/homepage_news.aspx?res=P_CORP.

Sights and Sounds

For all of its deficiencies, India is an absolute joy as a travel destination. It's a mind-blowing, mind-numbing country to visit. You literally do not know what you will see around the next corner. In Delhi, it could be street urchins putting on an acrobatics show for a few rupees. In Mumbai, it could be a colorful wedding ceremony. In Jaipur, it could be a festival marking the end or beginning of one of the many religious holidays complete with elephants and camels decked out in all manner of paint and precious metals. In Allepe to the south, you can meander down backwaters in an intricately carved houseboat, while at the Amber Fort you can ride an elephant to the gates and take a jeep back down. In Cochin, fisherman still cast the same nets their ancestors cast a thousand years ago, while on Elephanta Island, near Mumbai, you can be carried up the steps on a palanquin to see Hindu temple ruins dating to the fourth century. Many of these are riddled with bullet holes after being used by the Portuguese for target practice in the 1500s. In Udaipur, you can spend glorious nights at the Lake Palace Hotel, a hotel built in the middle of a man-made lake, and watch elephants bathe in the lake. You may recognize the hotel as the backdrop in the James Bond film *Octopussy*. And, even after visiting India a few times, you will barely scratch the surface. I have yet to visit the hill stations like Darjeeling or tiger preserves such as the Royal Chitwan National Park across the border in Nepal. A major destination country, India boasts thousands of miles of tropical coastline, none more famous than the beaches in Goa, where many hippies from the 1960s made the Indo-Portuguese coast infamous.

However, there is one place in India that draws more than 2.4 million tourists a year: the Taj Mahal. It is as magnificent as you have imagined it to be. Perfectly symmetrical, this architectural wonder is an easy two-hour train ride from Delhi. The grounds are easy to walk about and the monument is wide open to visitors all year round. The Taj is located in Agra, not the prettiest of places as far as cities go. But, it is definitely a must-see on any trip. Plan to spend at least a day at this "mausoleum to eternal love" and then retire to the fabulous Oberoi Amarvillas for a cold drink on its massive verandah overlooking the Taj in the distance. It is one of the best hotels I have stayed at in India. You can find more information about the Oberoi at www.oberoihotels.com/oberoi_amarvilas/index.asp.

India is a shopper's mecca where bargaining is expected for any and everything whether at a shop or a street market. Silks and fabrics are great buys as are precious and semiprecious stones. Silk rugs, wooden carvings, inlaid knick-knacks, exotic saris, hand-painted prints, and, of course, spices are abundant everywhere. Most shops take credit cards, and U.S. dollars are also widely accepted. It can get overwhelming at times as the selection for just about any item is very deep. If you want something hand crafted and not machine made, India is your place. Sweat is cheap here, cheaper than China, and work is sought after in every corner. In the bigger cities like Mumbai you will find the best quality fabrics and the most current fashions, usually dictated by the Bollywood set. In places like Rajahstan, you will find sapphires and Lapis (from Afghanistan). Gold is available everywhere and usually it is 22 carat and never less than 18 carat. Buying gold jewelry in India is perhaps the best bargain of all, as you are often paying only based on weight and not for design. Be careful though, gold paint is cheap. Almost any item can be shipped to the United States or any other address, and I have had several items—big ones—shipped to me without any issues.

Unlike China, India is a democracy with very liberal stances on everything from freedom of expression to religion. While a majority Hindu country, all religions, races, and faiths are not only tolerated but encouraged. Of course, there are periodic fallouts among religious extremists of all types. One has to note that there are more faiths represented in India than any other country in the world. It is a true melting pot in that sense. It is a good idea to read up on the different places, especially the temples you are planning to visit. Each group has its idiosyncrasies and while it is very hard for a tourist to offend someone in the country, the better option is to be well informed.

There are two ways to travel to and within India. One is on your own and this is perfectly safe. English is very, very widely spoken, as India was a former British colony. You will be accosted by beggars and street urchins. Your best bet is to give out food and not money—I prefer the mini snack packs as they're easy to carry. If you get flustered easily or hate crowds, don't visit India. If you still must go, then do it with a tour group where you may enjoy the safety in numbers. I have had the pleasure of visiting India with a group and without. By far, one of the best organizers of tours to India (and China and many other exotic destinations) is Opportunity Travel, headed by a very close friend of mine, Barbara Perriello. If she does not have a trip scheduled, she can put one together through some of her contacts. Opportunity Travel specializes in relatively high-end travel programs, something you will be eternally thankful for after your visit. You can contact Barbara at barb@opportunitytravel.com or visit her web site at: www.opportunity-travel.com/.

Strengths

India is a democracy, the largest one on the planet. It has an established legal code, a well-functioning banking system, and a history of commerce. The country has a huge, educated population that is English speaking. The government in power today is more pro-business and pro-foreign investment than at any other time. The political climate is also stable and the electoral process is not a mystery. While road infrastructure is challenged, the country has a good network of airports, railways, and ports.

The country has a major geographical advantage located as it is in the heart of Asia with easy access to the Middle East and Africa via the Indian Ocean and to China via land, and Australia and Indonesia for resources. Its forte is technology, and Indian companies benefit from dominance in the IT arena.

The well-educated population is cheap by global standards and offers a huge skill set, including English fluency. The country also has a massive population of laborers, who populate its factories at a very low cost, making ventures in India highly competitive and potentially very profitable. India is not considered a global threat militarily although it does maintain a large army and air force.

India's expatriate community is huge and very skilled. Its professional class can be found all over the world and thrives in middle- to upper-class society wherever its members settle in the West. They are now beginning to focus on their home country—exporting their ideas and skills back home. This has allowed India, like China, to accelerate both in terms of growth and innovation by taking some of the best ideas and trying to incorporate them into Indian society at large.

Weaknesses

India is, by most measures, overpopulated in relation to its resources. The vast majority of its population is reliant on locally produced foodstuffs and that means an over reliance on weather patterns like the monsoon season. Parts of the country have a history of droughts and famine when the rains do not come.

India does not have a good infrastructure apart from the ones mentioned previously. Roads are terrible at best and transportation, while cheap, is not pleasant. There are tolls roads, which are better, but the country is sorely lacking a good highway system.

While India is a peaceful country for the most part, it does share a very volatile border with Pakistan, and constant fighting over the beautiful Jammu/Kashmir region often scares the rest of the world, as both India and Pakistan are nuclear nations. India also shares a border with China and while there have been conflicts in the past, most observers do not believe either country is interested in pursuing that type of relationship.

India has also been the target of several terrorist attacks in the past few years. This is the result of conflicts with Pakistan and also the relatively lax security that is prevalent across this country where petty theft and tribal issues are the norm.

While a huge part of the population is educated and progressive, India does have a large population that is illiterate and, for lack of a better word, backward. This has resulted in a wide chasm between the haves and have nots, something that is common to all emerging markets.

India has a poor power grid, and power supply is not reliable in many areas. This is due to aging systems and a growing population that is consuming more and more power. It is not unusual to find villages with inadequate power. Drinking water is another problem. Foreigners cannot drink the water in India; and be very, very sure that even your bottled water is from a trusted supply—get it at the hotel before you venture out. Diseases common to tropical climates have not been eradicated, either. In a sense, there are two Indias: one that is thoroughly modern and one that still feels like it belongs in the twelfth century. Fortunately, India's religious and social mores allow for harmonious coexistence. That may change though. India's caste system is also a problem, as it tends to marginalize a huge chunk of the population just because of the misfortune of being born to the wrong caste.

Yes, the caste system is alive and thriving despite efforts by the government's public relations arm to play it down. Open any Indian paper and you will see personal advertisements that are trying to match make an "upper caste Brahmin boy" to an "upper caste girl." This represents a weakness because it does not allow the population to fully benefit from India's growth and success, something that may go from weakness to threat.

India's stock market is well established. It's the oldest in Asia and functions well. As in most emerging markets, it does not have the liquidity to absorb massive foreign investment. And, as I noted earlier, market manipulation can occur. This is true in any market; however, in smaller markets the effects can be more pronounced. The Indian market is also very volatile. While there are more than 5,000 companies that trade on the Dalal Street exchange, fewer than 10 percent of them make up more than 80 percent of the capitalization. When there is a panic, try to imagine a herd of elephants trying to squeeze through a set of French doors and the resulting chaos.

While the Indian government has been trying to adopt a very pro business and pro foreign investment stance, it has run into issues that are hard to resolve. India has a very, very established labor and business contingent. Many of the trades are controlled by families or clans that date back to before the Mughal times. For example, in Mumbai, commercial establishments use Dhobiwallas to do their laundry (Dhobi is derived from the word wash). These

Dhobiwallas occupy a massive outdoor laundry facility that is in itself a sight to see in Mumbai. They not only work there, but they live on the premises as well. Like a trade union, they don't take any prospect of modernization lightly.

India's business community also benefits from the past policies of isolationism. Since the country was never a massive importer of foreign goods, it never liked the prospect of opening its doors to foreign companies or competition without exacting a very high price. That same mentality exists today. Companies like French supermarket giant Carrefour or U.S. powerhouse Wal-Mart have not been able to open retail operations in India as of the summer of 2011. The rules are easing, but both companies will have to make major investments before they will be allowed to operate if at all. Both companies have spent more than a decade trying to convince the government to let them operate a retail store. The main opposition lobby is the millions of shopkeepers that run tiny little businesses in every neighborhood in the country. It's not about progress, it's about competition and Indian business is not fond of external competition.

Poverty is a major issue for India. It is a problem that has to be addressed before the country can move forward. India's per capita annual income is less than $1,400. A huge percentage of the population, more than 500 million people, live on less than $2 per day. Even when measured for purchasing power parity (the amount the same dollar buys in India versus a country like the United States) the number is still under $7 per day. That type of poverty is something you do not hear about in the business channels or the business community, but it exists and it's real.

Finally, corruption in India is an epidemic. But that is the same in every emerging market and many developed markets, too. It is a weakness, however, that prevents transactions from being completed, prevents projects from being completed on time, and in general saps the economy of growth.

Opportunities

India is where China was 20 years ago in terms of growth. That presents a compelling opportunity for many investors. The retail sector is huge with over one billion consumers. The infrastructure opportunity is the biggest in the world as it represents the country's greatest need. Agriculture is also a huge opportunity as much of the country's food supply comes from small farms that do not use modern mechanical or seed technology. The country boasts a massive, educated workforce that can be subcontracted by richer countries in areas like technology, pharmaceuticals, and industry. A relatively open society, India is also one of the world's largest exporters of entertainment. Bollywood dwarfs Hollywood in the number of movies it produces—almost double—and India is beginning to export its entertainment culture. By the same token, India is a huge potential market for incoming entertainment. Most families have or have access to televisions, and I can think of few countries I have been to where screen entertainment is such a popular pastime.

Threats

The greatest threat India faces is not being able to sustain growth. It has a massive agrarian population that is moving into the cities and taxing every possible resource from water to electricity. A massive, unskilled labor force dwarfs the skilled labor force and if reforms to the system are not achieved, then social unrest will be the order of the day. Already, there have been instances of major strikes and threats of shutdowns when the lower castes feel that their opportunities are being impugned by the upper castes. Among the huge, uneducated population, work stoppages and threats of violence are often adopted as a means to effect change.

Pollution is a major problem in the country. Like China, India is hugely reliant on fossil fuels and there are few regulations that protect the environment. In rural areas, disease and mortality are major issues. The rural population has also been slow to adopt birth control measures, and unlike China, which mandated birth control by fiat, India, as a democracy, has never been able to address the issue adequately through education. Overpopulation is as big a threat as any other in a country that can barely feed its population in the best of times.

While there are few internal political or social threats, one in particular does stand out. India is a majority Hindu nation and every so often Hindu nationalism rises to the fore. Instances of major violence are well documented between Hindus and Muslims and Sikhs. In 1984 for example, more than 500 (some estimates put it as high as 1,500) people were killed at the Golden Temple in Amritsar when Indian forces ousted militant Sikhs who took over the vast religious compound. The militants were protesting the disenfranchisement they felt they were suffering at the hands of the Hindu majority. Within four months of the massacre, Indian Prime Minister Indira Gandhi was assassinated by her Sikh bodyguards, leading to further bloodshed across India. While tensions between the Hindus and Sikhs has simmered down, tensions between Muslims and Hindus have picked up. Several terrorist attacks in the past five years, including two in Mumbai in 2009 and 2011, have been placed at the feet of Pakistani-backed Muslim separatists who look at the Jammu/Kashmir region as belonging to Pakistan. While neither country has come close to declaring an all-out war in recent years, border conflicts are common. Perhaps the only reason India has not invaded Pakistan, which it could do, is because both countries possess nuclear weaponry.

Isolationism is also a potential threat to India's emergence. If it does not liberalize policies allowing foreign companies more rights and more access to its markets, it could face a backlash. Companies like Coca Cola, India's leading soft drink until 1977, pulled out of the country when the new government ordered the company to turn over its formula and dilute its stake in the local franchise it owned. The company returned in 1993 when a new, more liberal government took over power. I recall on my visit in 1997, I could not get a Diet Coke anywhere in India and yet, just across the border in Katmandu I was able to get my fill. India must open its doors to compete on the world stage, yet it faces a major crisis at home if it does so too quickly. All emerging markets face this same threat, but if a country like India wants to become a first-tier emerging market, then economic reform must move at a faster pace than it is moving today. Right now, the country solidly occupies the second-tier space.

CHAPTER 3

Egypt

THE RISE OF NORTH AFRICA

As Egypt goes so goes North Africa and likely the Middle East. When I visited the country, just a few weeks after the Tahrir Square revolution, Egypt was still not going anywhere.

The decision to visit Egypt so soon after the revolution was not an easy one. My job requires me to be on the cutting edge of market events anywhere in the world. And Egypt was and is in the midst of possibly the greatest revolution of our time: the transformation of the Arab world. If it fails, the world will be a worse place to live in, with uncertainty in natural resource supply, religious intolerance, and the affirmation of cultural backwardation for hundreds of millions of people—women especially. My publisher, colleague, and friend Robert Williams called me on my phone. "We need to go to Egypt," he said. I answered, "Who's we?" Of course I knew who "we" was, but it was funny nonetheless. I had some contacts in the region and our goal was to get a feel for the country and its investment outlook. Egypt's proximity to major oil producing countries like Libya, Saudi Arabia, and other Gulf nations makes it the perfect place to visit to gather intelligence without having to wait a month for a visa or getting hit by an errant NATO shell aimed at a Libyan dictator.

Within 72 hours of our conversation I was at the airport. Then the problems began. Weather delays, mechanical problems, and two missed flights as a result, were going to put me on the ground in Cairo at close to 10 P.M.—not an ideal time to land in a country I last visited when I was 8 years old, not to mention the fact that a revolution was in full swing! The Egypt Air flight from Frankfurt to Cairo was nearly empty. I sat next to an elderly gentleman who was clutching his prayer beads tightly. I asked him his thoughts about what was happening. He was quite frank with his thoughts. Mubarak was a crook and Egypt is better off with his ouster. However, the only thing he was certain about other than that thought was the fact that he, his family, and his business faced only uncertainty for some time to come.

Egypt is one of a handful of countries in the area where you can purchase a visa on arrival. Signs are everywhere after you deplane and it's a painless process. The Egyptian pound is easy to buy at the airport and rates are fixed by the government. There were no lines at passport control or at customs. Prices for transportation to and from the airport are all over the place and a private car will easily set you back US$100. I opted for the Cairo shuttle bus from the airport for about 100 Egyptian pounds or $20. (You can find out more about the shuttle bus at www.cairoshuttlebus.com/.)

My driver, Mohamed (a popular name in the region), spoke English very well and definitely knew his way around random checkpoints that were set up between the airport and the hotel. As we drove through Cairo I was surprised to see that the city was functioning, meaning that lights were on in major buildings, there was traffic on the roads, and many shops were open. Was this a revolution in name only? As we approached the hotel, I noticed an absence of people walking on the sidewalks. In a city like Cairo, with its reputation for a lively population, this was unusual. I checked into the hotel and was politely escorted to my room with a warning not to wander the streets at night, even around the hotel. I wasn't going anywhere. My biggest fear, however, was unfounded—the hotel's high-speed Internet access worked perfectly!

Not Your Mummy's Egypt

When you think of Egypt you think of the pyramids, the Sphinx, the Nile, papyrus, an ancient civilization far advanced among its peers, a land of pharaohs buried in gold vaults, the Corniche at Alexandria overlooking the Mediterranean, the owners of the Suez

Canal connecting the Mediterranean to the Red Sea—you think of a country that has unlimited potential.

Then you arrive. You see a country where 40 percent of the population lives in poverty, abject poverty. Walk around Old Cairo and you will see that donkeys still pull carts of fresh fruits through the streets. Pollution creates a cloudy haze, traffic is a nightmare, and corruption is a way of life. Not the most romantic scene and one that most tourists don't witness.

My driver was a former driver for assassinated Egyptian President Anwar Sadat. He was in his 70s and knew the streets and side roads better than most, according to him. As a member of the older generation in Egypt he longed for the days of Sadat, "days filled with honor," when you could trust the country's leader. Days when the country's leader was not afraid to be in public because he had nothing to hide. Then came Hosni Mubarak, the now-deposed president who took over after Sadat's death. Mubarak looted and pillaged Egypt. He put friends and family in positions of power, lived a lavish lifestyle, and ruled with a dictatorial style using fear as his main weapon. The fear was generated by the actions of his secret police and intelligence service called the Amn Al-Dawla. Nothing really new here; it's the same way most of the countries in the region and in the Middle East are ruled. The Shah had his Savak and Saddam his Mukhabarat. Mubarak just followed the same script with one major difference. He allied himself with the United States and that provided benefits like foreign and military aid.

Egypt today is a mess, as it should be after more than three decades of one party/one-man rule. The military is the real power, but it faces a repressed public that is ready to turn against it if provoked. None of this takes away from one important thing that Egypt does have going for it: potential.

It still controls the Suez Canal, a passageway that shortens the time for goods passing from the Mediterranean Sea to Asia. The canal was completed in 1869 and eliminated the need for boats to navigate the seas around the African continent. But, it comes at a price. Ships pay an average of $250,000 to traverse the canal, adding more than $5 billion to Egypt's coffers annually. The strategic location of the Suez and the fact that many oil tankers cross it makes Egypt a strategically important country, as well.

Egypt is home to several of the Wonders of the World including the pyramids at Giza, the Sphinx, and the Valley of the Kings, and many other tourist hotspots. Its tourism industry is very well developed and contributes a further $12 billion of GDP (officially). When I was there during the high season, occupancy at hotels in Cairo was below 40 percent. Of course, it allowed me to enjoy a beautiful room at the Nile Kempinski overlooking the Nile, complete with superb butler service from Mohamed, my butler. Unofficially, tourism probably generates twice that amount given the emphasis on cash transactions and tips. In fact, what bothered me the most about Egypt were the constant tip requests from everyone. Unlike many countries outside the United States and some places in Europe, where tipping is completely discretionary and often not accepted, in Egypt it is not only accepted, it's almost a requirement regardless of the level of service and will usually be met with a look of disappointment regardless of the size of the tip. My advice is to ignore the looks and tip whatever amount you are comfortable with tipping—just know that you will receive the evil eye if you don't. Oh, don't drink the tap water. And, if you really want to indulge in a local delicacy, order the Oum Ali for dessert—especially at the Kempinski!

Egypt in general and Cairo in particular are relatively safe (except during revolutions, of course), and while I wandered markets and streets near the spectacular Al-Azhar Mosque and university alone, I would not recommend doing so without a guide during the current times. As for shopping, prices are cheap and your guide will undoubtedly take you to the shops that are the highest priced and offer him the greatest kickback, so be ready to bargain and don't be shy about it. Things that are popular include fabrics, perfumes, and, of course, papyrus. But, beware, not all papyrus is created equally and if that is your interest, do some research about how to buy it before you go.

A Stock Market Dilemma

It was early on a Monday when my contact at the Egyptian stock exchange, Mohamed Saeed, called me at the hotel and confirmed my meeting with the new chairman of the exchange, Mohamed Abdel Salam. I won't go over his background in depth other than to say he is an experienced market professional who has spent his time working in the industry. The EGX had just opened for trading after being closed for weeks.

My first impression of the exchange? Maximum security.

Submachine gun-wielding soldiers guarded the entrance, and an armored personnel carrier was parked ominously across the street.

My first question to Chairman Salam regarded the seemingly premature re-opening of the exchange just a few days earlier. He admitted being under extreme pressure to open, due to a deadline imposed by Morgan Stanley's index, which tracks emerging market shares.

You see, if the exchange hadn't opened that week, Egypt would have lost its spot in the index, triggering severe capital outflows. Given that inflows from foreigners have exceeded outflows since the exchange's inception, nobody wanted such a favorable trend to end.

Investing in Egypt is not easy for foreigners. Direct investment by individual non-Egyptians is next to impossible. But, you can invest through mutual funds and exchange traded funds. My favorite one trades in the United States under the symbol EGPT. It holds most of the blue chip Egyptian companies. See table 3.1.

Table 3.1   EGPT

EGPT Top Ten Holdings (data as of Aug. 3, 2011)	
1. Orascom Construction Industries SAE GDR (ORSD)	7.96%
2. Commercial International Bank Ltd	7.93%
3. Orascom Telecom Holding GDR (OTLD)	7.18%
4. Egypt-Kuwait Holding Co.	6.22%
5. Talaat Mostafa Group (TMG)	6.05%
6. Telecom Egypt S.A.E	5.85%
7. Efg-Hermes, Cairo	4.94%
8. Centamin Egypt Limited (CELTF)	4.64%
9. Juhayna Foods Industries	4.51%
10. National Societe Generale Bank	4.42%

Source: ETF Database, www.etfdb.com.

The top 10 holdings account for 60 percent of the ETF and there are only 28 companies in the ETF. Before investing, be sure to visit the site or that of the fund manager Van Eck for current holdings: www.vaneck.com/page_mv.aspx?Group=ETF.

Orascom occupies two of the top three spots in the portfolio. CEO of Orascom Telecom, Naguib Sawiris, was at the meeting I had at the exchange. He is a Coptic Christian (Copts make up 10 percent of the country's 80 million people) in a majority Muslim country—a testament to Egypt's religious tolerance. He and his family members control the Orascom companies, which are the largest private employers in the country. Of course, he was optimistic—what else could he be with his family's wealth at risk? He is quite a charming individual and well respected.

The ETF is quite volatile, a reflection of the general area and the current climate. But, in my opinion, it is the perfect proxy for both Egypt and the region in general. Egypt is the litmus test for North Africa and the Gulf Arab region. If it can emerge from its crisis as a true secular democracy, its success will be replicated regionally. If it fails, the region will likely remain in turmoil.

The country could be what Turkey is today. Turkey was not dissimilar to Egypt some two decades ago in terms of growth. Today, Turkey is a strong economic power in the region, a strong ally for the West—both militarily and economically—all the while remaining a religious country that operates within a strong secular framework that is guaranteed by a strong military. It's not perfect, but it's a darn sight better than most of the countries in the region when it comes to economic transparency, women's rights, and religious freedom.

It's important to remember, too, that while Egyptians are religious, the revolution was spurred by financial issues not religious ones. And until money starts flowing into the hands of Egypt's citizens—away from corrupt policymakers—for infrastructure projects, education, and tourism, Egypt will underachieve.

It certainly won't attain first-world status—an honor it held over 5,000 years ago when it dominated much of the civilized world—until this new government takes root. I left Cairo through Tahrir Square where the burnt out shell of Mubarak's National

Democratic Party was deserted, while across the street a new Ritz-Carlton was swarming with construction workers building Egypt's newest wonder.

Strengths

The Suez Canal. Tourism. A youthful workforce. A strong movement toward democracy as evidenced by the relatively nonviolent (to date) popular revolution. Strong agricultural sector. Good supply of internal energy with strong reserves of natural gas and hydroelectric power. Adequate infrastructure. A history of commerce with the rest of the world. Religious tolerance. An established stock exchange.

Weaknesses

Education is not reaching the masses, which will result in a less skilled workforce. There is corruption at all levels and a lack of foreign investment as a result of the revolution. Lack of government policy aimed at development of infrastructure, education, and social welfare in general. Poverty.

Opportunities

Development of tourism. Advancement of agricultural technology. A young population that could be the best educated in the region. Continued religious tolerance and freedom will allow for investment from the international community. Technology. Egypt is poorly wired for Internet service, although cell phones and TVs are everywhere. Construction—for a country known for its architectural prowess, it suffers from a lack of habitable structures in areas surrounding the city. Companies in Egypt are undervalued because of the risk associated with uncertainty. With some clarity, the market will double overnight. The ability for foreign individuals to invest through ETFs and funds.

Threats

Religious intolerance could develop quickly if the religious parties gain power. Women's rights could be diminished in such a scenario. The lack of a stable and established government could begin a trend of instability; the first government in power after a revolution is not always the best one. Human rights—the underpinnings are there, but the poor are treated very badly and they make up 40 percent of the population. Regional threats from unstable countries like Libya post Gadhafi. A break in ties with Israel, one of its neighbors, could sow the seeds of new conflict in the region. A closure of the stock exchange would be catastrophic for investors as any confidence built would be lost for much longer this time.

4

Vietnam

THE TIGER CUB OF ASIA

China is the Asian tiger. It will grow for many more years before its story is finally told. But, if it's real growth that you are looking for, you need to look just a few hundred miles away toward Vietnam. I liken the country to a tiger cub, tucked safely away near its mother, but with much more growth ahead.

The funny thing about Vietnam is that there is still a big difference between the North and South even though it is again one country. Hanoi, the capital, is so close to the Chinese border that I couldn't get on Facebook while I was there. Now, the only other place I know where Facebook is unavailable is China. If you really want to know who the boss is in the region, you have your answer.

Hanoi is not a very attractive place in the winter. It's cold, damp, and cloudy. And, it's a pretty boring place unless you are into eating endless bowls of noodles and practicing a suicidal version of jaywalking. There are a few museums, lots of restaurants, a beautiful lake in the middle of town, and a token high-end shopping district. There are lots of memorials and statues of Ho Chi Minh, the Marxist revolutionary leader who was instrumental in the creation of the Democratic Republic of Vietnam (it was neither) after World War II and the Peoples Army of Vietnam. He played a major role in the Vietnam War until his death in 1969. He is so revered that the government changed the name of Saigon in the South to Ho Chi Minh City in 1976. Many people still refer to it as Saigon, however—it has a better ring to it.

Looking out of my window from the Hanoi Hilton (yes, there is a real Hilton in Hanoi, and I am not referring to the prison nicknamed the same) I could see the opera house built in classic French style and modeled after the Palais Garnier opera house in Paris. It's in excellent condition and, like the Hilton, is at the heart of the city. I would strongly recommend the location for any visit. The most surprising thing I saw from my window was something not native to Vietnam, a Bentley Continental GT. The same car costs about $180,000 new in the United States; in Vietnam, it probably cost twice that amount. It was parked in front of a set of wrought iron gates, next to a Porsche Cayenne. Now, these cars are a dime a dozen in places like Singapore, but that's to be expected since the per capita income in Singapore is north of US$44,000 per year (compared to the $47,000 in the United States). But, in Vietnam, the per capita income is right there above Moldova . . . around $3,400 per year!

When I see things like the Bentley in a third-world country, it catches my attention. Now, Hanoi and Saigon are really not like your average third-world dumps (Managua firmly occupies that space in my mind). They have beautiful city centers, lots of neon-covered high rises, good streets, great restaurants, lots of shopping, and very nice people. But, they are third world as far as economic development is concerned—that's also where the opportunity lies.

Vietnam's recorded history goes back some 2,700 years—it's been around for a while. It's long had a relationship with China and was actually under Chinese rule for many hundreds of years from 236 BCE to around 938 CE. Since that time it has remained mostly independent, although the Chinese, the Mongols, and the French have retaken or colonized the country on several occasions. In the end, none ended up keeping Vietnam, and the country has been fiercely independent since the French were defeated in 1954. The same spirit and ability to resist domination by superpowers is now manifested in the will of the new Vietnam to succeed on the world stage as an economic up and comer. Now, Bill Gates and Warren Buffett are worth more than Vietnam's 2010 gross domestic product just to put things in perspective for a moment. The same can be said for many other small countries. But, what sets Vietnam apart is its proximity to China and the work ethic of the population. If I had to make a bet on the one emerging market that will succeed in the long term and make the transition from Tier 2 to Tier 3 in the next decade, Vietnam would top that list.

Long Days, Hard Work, and Education

There is a pattern for success amongst the Vietnamese who want to succeed. It's not dissimilar to the formula for success embraced by people all over the world who want to succeed. It's a combination of a strong work ethic, education, and the will to succeed. There are a lot of places that fit the Vietnamese profile as a small third-world country, but they will never succeed because there is not a spirit of avoiding failure. My contacts in Vietnam introduced me to many people from all walks of life—older folks who survived the Vietnam War and the 20- and 30-somethings of the younger generation. The older generation has suffered the worst that the country's Marxist system and the ravages of war can bestow on a population. You see them working still, but besides being extremely friendly to foreigners, especially Americans, they are resigned to living out their lives in much the same fashion as they did over the past few decades.

The younger generation is different. They have tasted from the fountain of capitalism and heard the buzz that is spreading like a wildfire across Asia. China might border the North, but it is Thailand that borders the South, and Thailand is anything but a sleepy neighbor. This generation is all about succeeding. It can be intimidating to watch. They wake up early, work hard at jobs that aren't particularly glamorous, live with a polluted climate, ride around on scooters with at least one other person on board, and then, after work, they go to school. The field of choice is information technology.

Hustle and Flow

If you visited either Saigon or Hanoi and not both, you'd come away with the completely wrong impression of Vietnam. The two cities, and the North and South could not be more different. As I wrote, Hanoi is a grey place, especially in winter, both in terms of weather and personality. It's southern counterpart, Saigon, is not. It's sunny, hot, and lively.

Hotels with rooftop bars, karaoke music, cold beers, and loud company abound. Saigon was the refuge for U.S. servicemen during the Vietnam War, and many of the bars in the city that date back to that time are frequented by veterans making the trip back—I met several during my visit there. It's a happy place laced with sad memories.

The South Vietnamese were not fond of the communists from the North. They embraced a much more freewheeling lifestyle. It shows in the daily flow of traffic and life in Saigon. The day starts early, for sure, but the hustle and bustle is much more carefree and less regimented than in Hanoi. There are many beautiful hotels that line the Saigon River, which runs through the city. From my window at the Renaissance Saigon, I could see a beautiful skyline dotted with small skyscrapers, pleasure boats and barges navigating the river, and merchants plying their wares to the tourists walking along the developed boardwalk. Around the corner from the hotel about a block away, a high-end nightclub called Apocalypse Now was banging out tunes while the bouncers stood guard at the entrance. A few blocks further away there's a Hard Rock Café that is set in an upscale plaza on Le Duan Avenue. Saigon rocks!

To get around Saigon is an adventure in itself. Scooters rule. Many of the side streets are narrow and pedestrian traffic and rickshaws are the second most dominant form of navigation. Beware though: Traffic will not stop for you and if you are crossing the street, the last thing you want to do is stop dead in your tracks. You will be hit. The drivers and scooter riders are counting on you to keep moving and they will navigate their vehicles around you, not vice versa. It's an adrenaline rush that I repeated many times during my visit.

Hyper Growth

Lying in the shadows of China, bordering bustling Thailand, and next to emerging Cambodia, Vietnam occupies the sweetest spot in the region. It is nowhere near as developed as Thailand but much further ahead than Cambodia or even Laos. It has a massive coastline (almost 2,000 miles); huge, navigable rivers; fertile land; and easy road access to its neighbors. It has a hardworking population that is interested in education.

Over the past decade Vietnam has grown at between 6 and 7 percent per year. GDP in 2010 came in just north of $100 billion, a number that is projected to quadruple over the next 15 years. One can easily see where the growth is coming from: exports. Vietnam's exports totaled more than 60 percent of its GDP, and those exports—things like rice, fabric, electronics, and even crude oil—found their biggest home in the United States, followed by Japan and then China. Those countries will continue to dominate the export horizon, but their order will shift. Vietnam's biggest import partner is China, and I believe China will also become the country's largest export partner within five years.

China needs Vietnam more than Vietnam needs China. While Vietnamese inflation has been out of control recently, approaching the mid teens, that is a consequence of high growth and increasing consumption locally and easy money that has financed the growth. It is not unusual in the least for countries that are doubling their GDP every five to seven years to have high inflation. The key is for the inflation to show signs of moderating after a few quarters of hyperinflation; otherwise, a major recessionary period will set in as governments impose strict policies to curtail growth. The biggest pain suffered in Vietnam has been by investors who have seen the stock market plunge by as much as 75 percent from its highs to current levels. And the currency, the dong, has depreciated by 25 percent in five years versus the U.S. dollar. Yet, the future for this socialist country remains extremely bright if forces that contributed to inflation can be moderated. The one thing that cannot be stopped is the growth that has led to massive declines in poverty in the country.

China is getting expensive by third-world manufacturing standards. Its growth has outstripped that of even Vietnam, and that is for a country that measures its GDP in trillions not billions. A result of China's growth is an increase in living standards, higher wages, and higher costs. Now, some of the business that found a home in China, particularly manufacturing, is moving to places like Vietnam—even Chinese businesses are setting up shop across the border. In 1999, China had 76 projects in Vietnam with a total investment value of $120 million. In 2009, that number was almost

700 and the value exceeded $2.5 billion. Early Chinese projects were focused in areas like hospitality and consumer products. Today, more than 70 percent of the projects are in the manufacturing sector. That trend will continue for the foreseeable future. China will have no choice but to engage its much smaller neighbor, and Vietnam will gladly accept the crumbs that fall from the Chinese tables. That is what makes Vietnam a compelling investment opportunity—the most compelling in my opinion—in the region. My optimism is only enhanced by the fact that Vietnam's stock market has plunged and many companies' stocks can be had for half price or less. The Vietnam ETF (NYSE:VNM), which I mentioned earlier, is by far the easiest way for nonlocals to invest in the country.

But, if you are looking for a local way to invest, perhaps in the manufacturing sector or in real estate in places like Saigon, you must do your due diligence. Laws do exist, but experience has taught me that laws really don't mean much when your money is tied up more than 8,000 miles away in a country where the language barrier is huge, the government is corrupt, and the investing dynamic changes daily. Vietnam is not a first-tier emerging market, or a second-tier emerging market. It is still a third-tier market that is on the cusp of becoming a second-tier market. What's holding it back is the lack of transparency in the legal system, the markets, and from the government, and also the lack of investment options for foreigners.

Ha Long Bay

A visit to Vietnam would not be complete without a trek out to Ha Long Bay, about a three-hour ride from Hanoi. Ha Long Bay is a UNESCO World Heritage Site—a designation that usually means that the place is something special. Not always. But, in this case, I am thrilled to tell you that it is one of the most fabulous places to not only visit but to spend a few days lazily exploring in a luxurious houseboat.

The road to Ha Long is quite interesting. It is a two-lane highway that is prone to traffic jams and accidents. A three-hour trip can easily be double that with just one accident on the road. But even then, it's worth the trip. Along the way you'll see hundreds of roadside stands selling freshly cored sweet pineapple—a perfect snack at about a dollar for a whole small pineapple. Coconut milk fresh from the husk is another treat.

One of the things that you will notice is that the Vietnamese only paint the front of their homes. Many homes are multifamily (the same family) and rise up a story each time more people move in. The houses are usually quite narrow but very ornate. The reason they only paint the front is because there is so little room between the homes that side windows are few so painting the sides would be a waste of money and paint since most people only look at your home from the front. The first floors of most homes, especially on the main roads, are little shops. They all sell the same goods: chips, cookies, and other dry packaged goods. There must have been at least a thousand of them between Hanoi and Ha Long Bay.

A word about the people. We were delayed by an accident on the way to Ha Long. Quite a few members in the group I was traveling with needed to use restrooms. We approached a small shop owner and he graciously allowed many to use the bathroom in his house. Of course, his generosity was well rewarded as we cleaned out most of his stock of chips and cookies to sustain us for the rest of the ride! He was as pleasant and polite as all of the people I met on my trip. It is a culture of hospitality and foreigners are treated with great respect and kindness. I was surprised, honestly, considering the number of occasions where foreigners had devastated the country through war.

Ha Long Bay (Descending Dragon Bay) contains a series of mountainous outcroppings (limestone karsts) that jut out of the water. These aren't just little rocks, but little islands dotted with small mountains some of which are more than 100 feet high—and there are more than three thousand of them! The houseboats, rowboats, and sailboats navigate through the misty channels stopping at some of the 500-million-year-old structures so that visitors can disembark and explore the hollows and caves, which feature some of the most breathtaking stalactites and stalagmites I have ever seen. One cave in particular (don't worry, you'll be taken there by your guide) is so large that the government has set up a light show inside it, and it can accommodate several hundred people at a time.

Once back on the boat you can feast on local seafood delicacies to your heart's desire. Along the way numerous little boats will approach with hawkers selling everything from fresh fruit to costume jewelry—the fruit is cheap, the jewels are extremely over-priced by local standards. Wait until you get to the markets in Saigon to buy or better still, if you're headed to China, you'll find everything at the Pearl Market in Beijing for a tenth of the price.

Vietnam is a land of many wonders, both geographic and economic. It will be a major player in Asia given time. Along the way, the market will crash (as it currently has) and provide the astute investor an opportunity to trade Vietnam for significant gains. A move back to the old highs would result in a gain of more than four times invested capital, and it's something I feel will happen again within the next five years.

Strengths

The country has a young population that is eager to learn and to work. Its proximity to China, Laos, Cambodia, and Thailand is a plus. It is self-sufficient in many respects, including agriculture and energy. The country has a history of perseverance and the ability to bounce back from crises of horrific proportions. A market and exchange system that tends to work well for a third-world emerging market. The ability for foreigners to invest, albeit through indirect channels. Infrastructure that is taxed but works. Strong sense of hospitality toward foreigners.

Weaknesses

Corruption exists in all ranks of government. Vietnam has a weak per capita GDP and a centralized planning system that is still run by the Communist Party. Housing for the massive urbanization that is taking place. Issues with neighbors like China regarding territorial boundaries. Dependence, for now, on the regional success of its neighbors.

Opportunities

Manufacturing. Vietnam has the capacity and manpower to take on projects that would once have gone to China but are finding a home in a cheaper place. Tourism is vastly underdeveloped, and the country is only beginning to exploit the thousands of miles of coast and river lines. The market is cheap by historical standards and that provides a place for foreign investors to allocate some capital, which will eventually find its way down the chain.

Threats

Inflation is now rampant and that could result in social unrest. Prices are on pace to double every four years while incomes are lagging that rate significantly. The ruling party is corrupt and that is impeding growth and encouraging the existence of a massive black market for goods and services. The country lacks a tax structure for public works projects. Threats from China regarding territorial boundaries could escalate, though this is doubtful. China is the major player in the region and influences the Hanoi government in matters of social policy—one has to remember that China played a major part in the support of North Vietnam during the Vietnam War, and the history of both countries has seen numerous instances of both cooperation and hostility. Old ties are hard to break. Vietnam could also suffer competitive threats from Cambodia and Laos at some point; however, in the regional pecking order, it's China first, then Thailand, and then Vietnam. Laos and Cambodia are a very distant fourth and fifth.

CHAPTER 5

Cambodia

LAND OF THE EIGHT-HAND MASSAGE

Flying into Siem Reap, Cambodia's second largest city, was an uneventful one-hour flight from Hanoi. The Vietnam Airlines plane was packed in coach, but only one person sat in the first class cabin. Cambodia is a very poor country, still recovering from the ravages of a civil war that lasted until 1998. It's a very small country as well, with fewer than 15 million people, 96 percent of whom are under the age of 65. More than 10 percent of the population perished between 1975 and 1998 under the hands of the communist Khmer Rouge government led by the infamous Pol Pot. In 1978, Vietnam pushed into Cambodia and occupied it for 10 years leading up to a civil war that lasted until the country, with outside help, was able to organize elections that finally led to Cambodia's independence from the Khmer Rouge. The country was left a devastated mess mired in unimaginable poverty. Consider that today the per capita income for a Cambodian is just over $760 per year, ranking it just ahead of Haiti for purposes of comparison. The country produces very little in the way of natural resources—not that it's a heavy consumer at $760 per head in income. Most cars in the United States consume more that $760 in gasoline per year.

For perspective you must understand the history of Cambodia. The Khmers, the indigenous peoples of the country, once ruled over Cambodia, Vietnam, Thailand, Malaysia, Laos, and Burma (Myanmar). The wealth that was produced as a result of the rule

83

contributed to the building of massive and ornate temple complexes like Angkor Wat in Siem Reap.

Knowing that Cambodia was a poor country, I was prepared to see the type of poverty that exists in the slums of India, Africa, and Central America. Granted, Siem Reap is the destination of choice in Cambodia because of the Angkor Wat temple complex . . . $760 is $760. I had an inkling that I could be wrong about Cambodia, however. That inkling occurred a few weeks prior to my trip when I was applying for visas. On this trip, I spent time in Singapore, Thailand, Vietnam, and Cambodia. I didn't need a visa for Singapore or for Thailand. For Vietnam a visa is required and it has to specify exact entry and departure dates or you *will* face a hassle at the airport. You can purchase a Vietnamese visa at the airport, as long as you have applied for it in advance with the consulate but have not received it. However, this, too, will be a hassle at the airport and you should be prepared to grease some official palms upon arrival to expedite the process. Also be ready to be grilled and intimidated. My advice? Get it ahead of time! For Cambodia, and I must admit this truly impressed me about the country, you can get a visa online in 24 hours just by visiting the consular website and sending them a digital photo and a $25 online payment. Alternatively, you can purchase a visa upon arrival from very polite officials for the same price with about a five-minute wait.

I arrived in Siem Reap in the afternoon. The immigration process was quick and painless. The airport was brand new and beautiful. As soon as I landed I was able to access the Internet on my phone. I followed the signs to baggage claim and after a two-minute walk arrived at an area that was enclosed for the baggage but also open air if you wished to wait outside. Outside there were cafe tables with umbrellas and two bars serving beer, cocktails, and snacks you could enjoy while waiting for your bags or to pick up arriving guests. I have never felt so comfortable at an airport. It was mid-January, the so-called cool season. The temperature was 85 degrees Fahrenheit . . . but there was hardly any humidity—just perfect. My hotel had sent a car and within 20 minutes of landing I was being welcomed in the lobby of the Raffles Grand Angkor with a cool drink and scented washcloth for my face and hands.

The road to the hotel was not what I expected. Once we exited the airport property the shops began to appear. Traffic was light, the roads were excellent, the cars were new and instead of tuk tuks, there were new scooters with carriages attached to them. Along the way there were several four-star hotels, a ton of restaurants, and markets everywhere—and it was super clean. Before setting foot in the hotel, I knew that this was a place that I would return to for an extended stay.

Raffles is the high-end hotel chain in Asia. I have stayed at its property in Singapore (where the infamous Singapore Sling was concocted) and now at Siem Reap—both are excellent choices. The hotel occupies prime space across from a park that hosts a mini arts and crafts market, and it also occupies the biggest footprint of any hotel within the city limits. It's been there for decades and was untouched during the country's civil war. The facilities are excellent with everything you would expect from a five-star property. The food was excellent and, once again, getting connected to the Internet was painless from anywhere on the property.

What I failed to take into account about Siem Reap and Cambodia in general was that it is for all intents and purposes a brand-new country. Ravaged by war, the country had languished in a primitive state with no modern conveniences or facilities for more than 25 years. So, when Cambodia began rebuilding, it emerged bathed in the newest and latest technology from high-speed Internet access to security cameras and modern transportation systems. The online visa, the new airport, the citywide Internet access—these are just not things that you find in your run-of-the-mill emerging country.

Angkor Wat

My schedule permitted me to pay a visit to the Angkor Wat temple complex, about 20 minutes from the hotel. Again, I was impressed by the road to the complex—no potholes. Upon arriving at the complex I was directed to a ticket stall where the agent took my picture and produced a ticket/ID within seconds that had my picture and details of the visit and a map on the back, all attached to a lanyard. Disney could learn a thing or two! Then, it was a short ride to the actual complex.

Angkor Wat is not small. It comprises several buildings spread over 203 acres and it is nothing short of spectacular. The sandstone structures are ornate with miles of carvings throughout. Rising more than 180 feet into the air, the central shrine and its galleries are a masterpiece of construction. Keep in mind the complex was built during the first half of the twelfth century. It is one of the Seven Wonders of the World and a must-see on any trip to the region. Siem Reap is a 45-minute flight from Bangkok and about the same distance from Saigon, as well. My only mistake was not allocating enough time in the area to visit the dozens of other temple complexes. If you are a little more adventurous, you can take brief tours around some of the complexes (not Angkor Wat) on elephant back for a few dollars.

Developing an Index

I'm a tall man. When I travel, it's usually not a very comfortable experience until I get to my destination. I remember paying someone so I could sit in his exit row seat on a Garuda flight from Singapore to Bali. I could not physically fit into my assigned seat. The same was true on an Olympic flight from Athens to Istanbul—I could fit into that one but not without the risk of severely bruised knees.

After many years of traveling around the world, I have developed a routine of sorts that involves as many massages as possible in the countries that I visit. Of course, I am limited by cost. In Europe, more than one is usually out of the question. In places like Switzerland a good massage will set you back a couple of hundred dollars. But, in Asia it's a whole different ballgame.

One of the indices that I have followed for some time is called the Big Mac Index. It was developed as a way of measuring purchasing power parity amongst different countries based on a one-dollar Big Mac sandwich. For example, in the United States, a Big Mac costs around $3. In China, the same sandwich is about 40 percent cheaper. In France, it is about 40 percent more expensive.

The problem is that in places like Cambodia and Vietnam there are no McDonalds (or Starbucks, either, for that matter). So, I have developed my own index to give you an idea of the relative cost of a similar massage throughout the region on this itinerary. In Singapore, a good massage will set you back about $60, in Thailand, about $20. In Vietnam the cost is around $10 and in Cambodia around $5. The eight-hand massage, which I now regret not trying, was $20. Next time!

Making Money in Cambodia

If there is such a thing as a pre-emerging market opportunity, Cambodia gets my vote. As of mid-2011, it was still in the planning stages of opening a stock exchange. It will likely happen sometime in 2012. There are companies, of course, that do business in Cambodia, usually with the blessing of the royal family, which rules the country. Among the early-stage companies that are accepting private capital are those in the banking and beverages sectors. One such company, called Kingdom Beer, recently accepted an investment of US$2 million from a private equity group in exchange for a majority stake. (I discuss the company in more detail shortly.) Granted, it's a small brewer of high-end beers, but it shows you the types of ground-floor opportunities still available.

Banks, power companies, seafood processing plants, real estate, hotels—you name it—Cambodia needs investment in all of these ventures and it is open for business. Most of the business is conducted in Phnom Penh, the capital city. Siem Reap, where Angkor Wat is located, was once a capital city but is now the tourist mecca of the country.

Because of the limited opportunity to invest directly in Cambodian companies through a stock exchange, one has to either invest directly on the ground or invest through private equity groups. I met with one such group and the managing partner of that group, Douglas Clayton. I'm not one to jump into any situation like this without getting a look at the eyes of the person behind any private deal—a lesson I've learned through experience. Still, there is no safety net when investing in a country like Cambodia or through any equity group. This is frontier investing at its finest.

I have met with Doug several times. He moved his entire family to Cambodia to focus his efforts on the region. That's dedication if you ask me. Cambodia is very nice . . . but not *that* nice. Doug knows the country, the people, and the businesses that he invests in. Still, it's a 5- to 10-year slog at best before you'll see the types of monster returns that can occur when you get in this early. Frankly, most people are just not interested in that time frame and risk. Not to mention the fact that you will need to pony up some serious cash to participate—$100,000 will get you in the door . . . if the fund is still open.

If you are interested in learning more about investing in Cambodia with Doug's company, Leopard Capital, contact him by visiting the website (www.leaopardasia.com). Leopard is also investing in places like Sri Lanka (Tier 2) and Laos (pre-pre-emerging).

Cambodia is an up-and-coming emerging market. It has a ton of upside based on where it is today and where it has come from. It's like a new country. It's almost at Tier 3 status. However, it could turn back the clock in a heartbeat if things were to fall apart, not like the days of the Khmer Rouge, perhaps, but to a dictatorial monarchy. I would say that there is a 10 percent chance of this happening. The country is doing well in many ways. Its economic growth and outlook are very good, but like everything else in Cambodia, old memories must be dealt with.

Strengths

A very young population, eager to learn and adapt to a capitalist model. Great telecommunications infrastructure; strong cellular-based technology. Strong "wonder of the world" tourism potential. Angkor Wat and Siem Reap can probably handle two to three times the number of annual visitors they currently attract. Proximity to Thailand, Laos, Vietnam, and China give the country longer term trade potential. Freedom of Internet.

Weaknesses

Early-stage nation building still in effect. Ravages of the civil war will take a long time to heal. Many places in the countryside are still off-limits because of landmines. The government is fond of nepotism and wants a piece of the action on all deals. There is a current lack of publicly traded vehicles for investors. No means to verify the books. Lack of a tax base or tax collecting mechanism outside of the big companies. This will hamper public sector growth and spending on things like roads. Water is not potable.

Opportunities

Tourism development. Infrastructure development. Ground-floor-type opportunities for those with access and capital. Increased trading opportunities with neighbors.

Threats

The country could fall back into dictatorial rule if the economy goes south. Child prostitution and human trafficking need to be addressed. Minefields need to be cleared completely or tourism will not thrive. During the civil war more than 13 million landmines were planted throughout the countryside. Thanks to international efforts, more than 12 million have been found and disabled. My advice would be to stay in the car and not venture too far for a walk.

CHAPTER 6

Thailand

SO MUCH FOR POTENTIAL

Thailand is possibly the best positioned to be a Tier 1 emerging market. It has a strong capitalist bent, a functioning and established stock market, decent infrastructure, a world-class metropolis in Bangkok, a booming tourism business, a strong port system, and a friendly and welcoming population with a history of modern independence from foreign rule. I could have written the same thing 20 years ago.

Therein lies the problem and why Thailand may never gain Tier 1 status. For as long as I can remember, Thailand has been the one to watch in Asia. It has seriously underdelivered. I commented to an audience once that "some emerging markets will always be emerging," and I truly believe that Thailand is one of those.

There's a joke I use on occasion when talking about Thailand. It goes something like this: "What do the Thais call a coup? An election." Since 1932, Thailand has witnessed 10 coups and 7 aborted attempts. Most recently, in 2006, the government of corrupt billionaire Thaksin Shinawatra was overthrown and he was forcibly exiled. Shinawatra came to power on a Peronist, populist platform and proceeded to enrich himself and his cronies. But the story does not end there. Fast forward to 2011 and Shinawatra's sister Yingluck Shinawatra was elected prime minister, again running on a populist platform. Thailand, like many Tier 2 emerging countries has a history of faux political instability. I say faux because the instability in the system is actually expected, much like it is in Argentina. And, like Argentina, Thailand is a country split in two—the haves and the have nots. And, the have nots tend to vote more.

One Night in Bangkok

Thailand is one of the most predictable markets in Asia, however, and the tool to use is the Stock Exchange of Thailand (SET). Let me explain. Before I visited in 2011 the Western media was reporting on violence in the streets of Bangkok. The Thai red shirts, representative of supporters of Thaksin (few doubt that he is still calling the shots, albeit through his sister) wanted him back in power. To make their displeasure clear, they rioted in Bangkok resulting in harsh military and police response leading to many deaths. The opposition yellow shirts are supporters of whoever is against Thaksin and the Shinawatras. I did not make the decision to go to Thailand based on the news media reports but based on the reaction in the SET. It was stable and that's all I needed to see. Upon arriving at Suvarnabhumi Airport, I could clearly see that it was business as usual. Most of the rioting was occurring in parts of the city that I was not planning to visit and really in such small areas that even the rest of Bangkok's population did not seem worried about it. Now, in the past, when there were real mass riots in the streets and the government brought in tanks to squelch the protestors, the SET would plunge by 20 to 30 percent overnight. Of course, I also consulted with two of my friends who either lived or had family in Bangkok for good measure. They sounded the all-clear as well, despite media reports.

Bangkok is a fabulous city. It doesn't sleep. It has diverse neighborhoods populated by every possible ethnic group on the planet. Shops, stalls, restaurants, and, of course, the red light districts are full of people all the time. It's a safe city, as well, with little serious crime. The city has a great overhead light rail system that you must use to avoid the heavy traffic that is present at all times. A word to the wise: Use the bathroom prior to getting into a car. You will invariably get stuck for an hour or more in traffic on some days. The Chao Phraya River (loosely translated as the River of Kings or Dukes) runs through Bangkok before emptying into the Gulf of Thailand. It's quite wide and navigable by all manner of craft, including long riverboats that make for a great transportation option. I know this both from riding in them, which was a blast, and also from having watched a day's worth of activity from my room at the Shangri La in Bangkok, recovering from a rare case of food poisoning. Strangely enough, it was the first time that I have ever gotten sick on a trip anywhere. Worse still, I ate the tainted food in a Lebanese restaurant that my local friend and college classmate, Jay Werba, took my colleague Chris Pillow and me to for dinner. Thanks, Jay! Nobody else in our group got sick, which makes the whole situation even more baffling. Next time I am sticking to the delicious Thai food!

One night after dinner we visited one of the red light districts that Thailand is famous for. Of course, I did not partake in any illicit or illegal activity. On the way to Patpong (a district that is more oriented toward foreigners) the streets are lined with little stalls selling Viagra and Cialis. Patpong is named after the Patpongpanich family, who owns most of the property. It's located between Silom and Surawong Road and exudes a carnival-like atmosphere. Strip clubs and bars line the streets as far as the eye can see, and if you're a man, you will be tugged at incessantly by beautiful Thai girls inviting you to enter their establishments. They hang out in front of each joint in small posses, dressed alike, usually in Dallas Cowboy cheerleader-type outfits. Walking up and down the street are hawkers selling everything from fresh fruit to insects on a stick.

Of course, as part of my research, I had to spend some time at one of these clubs. Inside the good clubs, the surroundings are spotless. You are not pressured in the least to do anything or buy a hundred drinks. Most of the patrons are older Americans or Europeans. And, all of the girls are young and Thai, usually from the countryside. Prostitution is illegal in Thailand—at least that's the running joke. These businesses had no lack of traffic and the goal is ultimately for the girls to find a foreigner and ply her wares. It's not a secret and it's not done in some back alley. It was plain to see. We stayed for a couple of hours just to people watch—it was a sight I will not forget.

At 2 A.M. we hopped in a cab and headed back to the hotel. There are some cities where taking a taxi is an adventure unto itself. Bangkok is not one of those places. Unlike Istanbul or Athens where I am always on the lookout for supposedly broken or already running meters, Bangkok was quite normal. However, a female friend of

(Continued)

(Continued)

mine who was there a few days prior to me was not as complimen-
tary about being treated fairly outside of Bangkok when it came to
transportation. Female travelers who travel unaccompanied in many
emerging markets have said the same. It's always a good idea to
deal with reputable companies recommended by your hotel, even
if it costs more. Unless you can speak the language fluently, you will
find yourself in dire circumstances sooner or later.

The First Domino

I can remember it clearly. I was in my hotel room at the Regent
in Hong Kong (now the Intercontinental), when the news of
the collapse of the Thai baht came on the TV. It fell by more
than 20 percent in one session, and what was once thought to
be a localized currency issue for Thailand (the actual crisis for
the currency began in May of 1997 when Thai banks came under
speculative attacks by investors and Singapore came to its aid),
turned out to be much more than that. For years prior to the
collapse of the baht and the Thai economy, the country's banks
had loaned out billions to the investment community fueling a
speculative bubble, especially in real estate. When that bubble
burst, much like it did in the United States during the period
from 2007 to 2011, the markets broke under the weight of bad
loans and insolvency of the banks. The crisis spread to the rest
of Asia and when it was over, many countries found themselves
debtors to the International Monetary Fund, which bailed them
out to the tune of $40 billion, upon promises of strict austerity
measures.

Thailand and much of Asia suffered several years of
depressed economic growth until rebounding in the early part
of the next decade. Recapitalized and with stricter lending standards in place, the Thai economy rebounded and the country
went back to worrying more about politics. During the crash,
it was not difficult to buy Thai equities, as well as those of
Indonesian and Filipino countries, for discounts approaching
70 percent. If there is a lesson to be learned about emerging

markets, this is it: When they crash, they crash hard and they crash fast. Liquidity dries up overnight and market routs are the norm. That is the time to buy.

Today, Thailand is growing its GDP at a 4 percent annual rate. It's been doing so, on average, for the past five years. Per capita income is between $5,000 and $6,000 depending on the source you use. That puts Thailand far ahead of countries like India, China, Vietnam, and Cambodia but still not even close to developed nation status. But, and this is a big but, the black market is rampant in Thailand, Bangkok in particular, and many transactions are done in cash with no trail for the tax collector. It is the same for most emerging market countries, and it is a problem that will plague them for decades to come. Corruption is rife in Thailand and it comes from the top. Corruption in recent times hit its highest level under the first Shinawatra, with kickbacks of 5 percent or more on projects being the normal starting point.

Thailand's population base of some 67 million and its strategic location as a developed cargo port and hub have allowed it to become a substantial trading partner (in Asian terms) with many of the neighboring countries. Thailand's major export is rice. While not even close to being the largest producer (China and India are the two biggest, but most of it is for local consumption) it accounts for more than 28 percent of the rice exported globally. Tourism is extremely well developed, and Thailand's beaches and islands are world famous for their beauty and resort accommodations.

Investing in property and property-related companies has historically provided the best investment gains in Thailand, followed by bank stocks, telecom stocks, cement stocks, and food companies. Thailand is also one of the largest producers of after-market automobile and electronics parts, but those businesses are highly commoditized and face major competition from other Asian countries. In truth, the type of companies that you want to invest in are those that serve the local market. Thai company shares are not hard to purchase, and some trade as American Depositary Receipts in the United States. But, as with every other emerging market, you are better off waiting for a crisis in Thailand and buying a Thai fund such as the Thai Capital Fund (NYSE:TF), Thai Fund (NYSE:TTF), or the MSCI Thailand Investable Market Index Fund (NYSE:THD). My rule of thumb is to start buying in tranches when the discount to net asset value (for TF and TTF) increases to over 25 percent—it's like buying a dollar's worth of shares for 75 cents or less. You can get quotes for the net asset value and the discount to that value by visiting the Closed-End Fund Association website at: www.closed-endfunds.com/.

Strengths

Thailand has a history of independence and an outstanding location with access to rivers and oceans. It is located in the fastest growing region in the world with close proximity to China and India. It has a fully functioning stock exchange and is well-known to the West.

Weaknesses

There is much political uncertainty. Nepotism is rampant and the population possesses a questionable work ethic compared to neighbors. There is a lack of willingness to cross the divide to developed nation status. Poor tax collection. Bangkok, the largest city and the center for commerce, has an overburdened infrastructure. The cost of doing business is slowly pricing Thailand out of the emerging market category.

Opportunities

Thailand has the chance to be the regional powerhouse behind China. It either borders or is within an hour by plane of Vietnam, Cambodia, Laos, China, Singapore, Burma, Malaysia, and Indonesia. It has the potential for increased agriculture production—especially rice. Its tourism industry is strong thanks to ample shoreline and resorts in the South and historical cities inland.

Threats

Thailand's neighbors have less expensive workforces. Corruption is rampant and political discord common. The country has a strong populist movement and a history of coups as well as a poor reputation for upholding women's rights. Religious tensions are rising from the southern part of the country where separatists have been waging frequent uprisings. The country's inability to make the move to developed market status after decades of independence and trade with the rest of the world could ultimately hurt prospects for the Thai economy as hungrier regional competitors emerge.

CHAPTER 7

Turkey

KNOCKING AT THE DOOR

The Turks must be laughing at the events unfolding in the West. For such a long time they have been seeking acceptance into the European Union in order to be viewed as an equal partner with the West. They argue location, straddling both Europe and Asia on the map. They argue military cooperation as the biggest Islamic NATO member. They argue economy, as the owners of one of the fastest growing economies in the world. And, they argue Greece. If that bankrupt nation can be part of the eurozone, then why not Turkey? Well, the answer has been that Turkey was not ready economically to join the first-world nations. In truth, it has more to do with the West's lack of acceptance of an Islamic country into its fold. Of course, no one will ever say that publicly except for the Turks. Well, the last laugh, it appears, is for them to enjoy. As the eurozone falls apart thanks to countries like Greece, Turkey is looking pretty golden right now even with its problems, and problems it has.

Turkey is a Tier 1 emerging market. It's very well developed, as it should be. The Turks have played a major part in world history for over 2,000 years. Turkey's largest city, Istanbul, once known as Constantinople, was the seat of the Roman empire under Emperor Constantine, who was the first major emperor to embrace Christianity. It is in Istanbul that you will find the magnificent domed cathedral called Hagia Sophia, or Saint Sophia, the predecessor to future domed Catholic cathedrals, including St. Peter's in the Vatican.

There are few cities in the world that can compare to Istanbul. As you cruise down the Bosphorus from the Black Sea, you see the magnificent minarets of the massive mosques that dot the skyline. Built on numerous hills, like Rome, anyone viewing Istanbul from the sea for the first time is usually taken aback by its beauty. The Bosphorus empties into the Sea of Marmara, which then empties into the Mediterranean and the Aegean seas. Turkey occupies a very strategic location, bordering Syria and Iraq to the north, Georgia and Iran to the east, and Bulgaria to the west. It has been part of the major global trade routes as long as any written history has been recorded.

At the height of its modern history, Turkey was home to the Ottoman Empire, borne out of Mongol rule. The Ottoman Empire controlled parts of Europe, the Middle East, and North Africa from the fourteenth century until the beginning of the twentieth century, reaching the peak of its power in the sixteenth and seventeenth centuries. At odds with the Catholic empires of Europe and the Austro-Hungarian empires for much of its modern history, the Ottomans fell from grace completely around the First World War. It was after this time that modern Turkey began to take shape. It did so, and successfully, by embracing a secular leader, Mustafa Kemal Ataturk, father of the Turks, who gained fame as a military leader. Ataturk vowed that Turkey would become a secular country with the backing of a strong military force dedicated to keeping it that way. Turkey also abandoned the traditional Turkish alphabet in favor of the Roman alphabet, further distinguishing itself from its Arab and Muslim neighbors.

But Turkey's modern history, while impressive under Ottoman rule, pales in comparison to its ancient history. It is in Turkey that you will find the magnificent ruins of Ephesus and Troy. It is where you will find the House of the Virgin Mary, where Saint John took her to spend her days until her Assumption. The Turks have played a part in history that few others can claim. Much of this is thanks to the Greeks who are not fond of the Turks—the feeling is mutual. They even share an island, Cyprus, over which they are constantly at odds, with the Greeks controlling one side and the Turks the other. Cyprus has been used by the European Union as a pawn in negotiations with the Turks in regards to entry into the EU—a moot point for now.

The Greeks and Turks have been at war for centuries. The Turks ruled Greece for almost 400 years from the fifteenth century until the early 1800s, under the Ottomans. It's a period of shame that the Greeks have not forgotten and territorial conflicts arise frequently between the two countries. It is also the Greeks who have put up major resistance to the Turks entering the EU. Yet, prior to the Ottomans, it was the Greek Byzantines who ruled the Turkish coast and Constantinople.

Istanbul

If you have a bucket list and Istanbul is not on it, you should add the city to it *tout de suite.* It is one of the world's major cities and one not to be missed. It is steeped in history, yet cosmopolitan at the same time. This city of 11 million does not sleep and offers visitors a wealth of sights and experiences. The best time to visit is in May or October when the crowds are small and the weather beautiful. Get a room overlooking the Bosphorus, the main waterway, and then be ready to explore. Istanbul is home to several palaces, the most famous being Topkapi Palace, home to the Ottoman rulers for 400 years before they moved to another palace, Dolmabahce, a more traditional European-style palace.

Istanbul is also famous for its mosques, which anyone of any faith can visit. Most famous of the mosques is the Blue Mosque or Sultan Ahmed Mosque, which is so named because of the blue tiles used throughout the building. A huge mosque, it is easily recognizable in photos by its size and its six minarets. It is one of only two mosques in Turkey with six minarets and unusual in the Muslim world since up until its construction only the Great Mosque in Mecca had six minarets. The Ottoman sultans solved this problem by adding a seventh to the mosque in Mecca.

It is located across from the Hagia Sophia, which, until the construction of the Blue Mosque, was the most venerated mosque in Istanbul despite its origins as a cathedral. Hagia Sophia is now open only for tourism and in itself is worth a visit to Istanbul. There are few places in the world that I have been to that are as captivating as the street between the two giant edifices, and not only for their symbolism. On a cool spring or fall evening the streets between are filled with vendors selling barbecued corn. The cafes are filled with music and one in particular is home to an exhibit of Sufi dancing. (Sufism is the mystical branch of Islam, whose adherents dance themselves into a trance-like state and are also known as the Whirling Dervishes.) The muezzin calls the faithful to prayer five times a day and the sound emanating from the mosque bounces off the giant dome of Saint Sophia. All the while, the sun is setting in the background over the Bosphorus.

The area is called Sultanahmet and is the oldest part of the city. There is an outstanding Four Seasons Hotel located in the neighborhood in a building that was formerly a prison. Let me assure you, no vestiges of the prison remain. The hotel has a terrace bar, which affords some of the best sights and sounds the neighborhood has to offer. Its web site is at www.fourseasons.com/istanbul/.

I have visited Istanbul a half dozen times over the years, and while this particular Four Seasons is one of the best hotels in the city, it has a lot of competition from the likes of the Ciragan Palace Kempinksi (www.kempinski.com/en/istanbul/Pages/Welcome.aspx), which is located on the eastern shore of the Bosphorus and boasts a magnificent view as well as spectacular Turkish baths.

There are hotels to meet every budgetary requirement and one in particular, Angels Home Hotel in Sultanahmet, offers good accommodations for the price and rooms with a view and an owner with an affinity for 1950s era Chevys, which he sometimes uses for airport runs.

Istanbul is a relatively safe city and one that is easily walkable—bring very comfortable shoes. I have observed that it is not a great city for women, especially European women, to walk unaccompanied. You will be approached by all manner of individuals. Of course, every nonlocal is approached by sellers of rugs who will invite you for a cup of tea or coffee and proceed to sell you overpriced rugs. It's best to say no firmly and walk away regardless of the number of attempts that will be made for your attention. It's not dissimilar to many other cities in the Orient in that respect.

Istanbul is a shopper's paradise with bargains to be had for gold, glazed tiles, silver, rugs, leatherwear, and spices. But, be prepared to bargain and walk away. The city has two main bazaars, the Grand Bazaar and the Egyptian Bazaar. Both are overpriced tourist traps so if you want to get a good price—and you can—take a local with you. The Grand Bazaar is a massive complex with thousands of shops, not stalls, located in a maze-like structure. It is something out of antiquity with nonstop haggling and every imaginable item for sale. After a while, every store might start to look the same—for good reason. On a given aisle there might be two dozen shops selling gold jewelry followed by another dozen selling silver. The Egyptian Bazaar, or Spice Market, is much less overwhelming in size but makes up for it with louder hawkers advertising Turkish Delight, a confectionary based on a gel of starch and sugar with a myriad of additives like dates or pistachios. The hawkers will try to get your attention by calling the product "Turkish Viagra." The Spice Market does have some of the best fruits, vegetables, and nuts in town, each piled high and extremely fresh and cheap. As for knickknacks, much of what is sold is unfortunately not even Turkish anymore as I found out by wandering in the back streets of the bazaar and noting the overwhelming number of empty boxes stamped "Made in China."

For more high-end shopping, Istanbul offers several large malls in its suburbs. But, within the city there is an area where the masses congregate: Istiklal Caddesi and Taksim Square. You can reach it by taxi or public transportation via the subway and a funicular. Taksim is great for shopping, dining, and people watching. But you will pay Western prices. At the end of Istiklal Caddesi, you can catch public performances of the Sufi dance at the Galata Mevlevi Monastery-Mevlevihane, something not to be missed. Be sure to check the schedule to see if it is open. There are other locations where you can watch performances, as well.

There are things you should be aware of when you visit Istanbul. The cab drivers are good, for the most part, but you will run across more than one who is crooked. Be sure that the meter is not running until you are in the car and see the driver turn it on. Public transport is excellent and very inexpensive, as are the taxis. Women should always carry a shawl or something to cover their heads and shoulders if a mosque visit is planned. You will be surprised at the diversity in appearance of the local populous. Turks come in all shapes and colors. Blonde and brown hair is as common as black hair. Blue eyes, green eyes—there is no one look. Turkish women are very liberated and miniskirts are not uncommon. However, I have noticed on recent trips that more women are wearing head (not face) coverings. This is a relatively new development and one that was frowned upon by previous governments. However, the current government, while probusiness and pro-West, does have a more religious bent. It is a new phase for Turkey and one that may signal a turning point for this once staunchly secular country.

Investing in Turkey

The Istanbul Stock Exchange has been around for about 25 years in its current form. But the first Turkish stock exchange was actually operating in the nineteenth century in the Ottoman court. The modern version is home to more than 320 companies, about two dozen of which can be traded on U.S. exchanges as American Depositary Receipts on the over-the-counter (OTC) exchange and the New York Stock Exchange. A list of these companies can be found on this site, which lists them by symbol and industry: www .site-by-site.com/adr/europe/adr_trk.htm.

A far easier way to trade Turkish stocks is to use a closed-end fund like the Turkish Fund, which has been around since 1989 (see Table 7.1). However, if you are going to use this route, then the rules of emerging market trading apply—wait for a crash and then buy and never buy at a discount of less than 25 percent. Keep in mind, when investing in foreign stocks that they trade during hours when most stateside investors are still sleeping. What happens overnight in a place like Turkey can have consequences, good and bad, on the following day in New York where the Turkish Fund (NYSE:TKF) trades. Since inception, the fund has returned an average of about 7.3 percent per year. That's quite unimpressive for an emerging market. That is why one needs to wait for opportunities. For example, during 2010, the fund returned more than 42 percent. Holdings range from cement companies to banks and breweries. I have visited the Efes Brewery and sampled the wares and can understand its strong presence in the fund's holdings!

Table 7.1   TKF Holdings

As of 30 June 2011	% of Portfolio
Adana Cimento Sanayii TAS A Shares	2.23
Akcansa Cimento AS	4.65
Anadolu Efes Biracilik Ve Malt Sanayii AS	9.22
Anadolu Hayat Emeklilik	1.61
Asya Katilim Bankasi AS	2.07
Cash	5.35
Coca-Cola Icecek AS	8.90
DO & Co. Restaurants & Catering AG	0.75
Haci Omer Sabanci Holding AS	3.38
Mardin Cimento Sanayii ve Ticaret AS	0.87
Net Other Assets	−0.12
TAV Havalimanlari Holding AS	2.51
Tofas Turk Otomobil Fabrikasi AS	1.76
Tupras Turkiye Petrol Rafinerileri AS	8.10
Turk Telekomunikasyon AS	9.55
Turkcell Iletisim Hizmetleri AS	3.62
Turkcell Iletisim Hizmetleri AS ADR	0.18
Turkiye Garanti Bankasi AS	16.23
Turkiye Halk Bankasi AS	3.82
Turkiye Sise ve Cam Fabrikalari AS	2.77
Turkiye Vakiflar Bankasi Tao Class D	4.66
Unye Cimento Sanayii ve Ticaret AS	0.93
Yapi ve Kredi Bankasi AS	6.96

Source: Morgan Stanley (fund manager) www.morganstanley
.com/msim/portal/site/US/template.PAGE/?msimPageTitle=
productdetail_us_fp_ii&u=86bb14f4dc87daf33d3afb1051a9e0
09&fund=1072.

Historically, very good gains have been made in Turkish stocks during periods of political unrest. While not in the same category as Thailand, Turkey does have a reputation for instability when it comes to politics. One of the main reasons for this is the struggle between those with a religious agenda and those with a secular one. Throw in a very active military sworn to protect Turkey's secular constitution and the possibility for volatility exists.

Turkey, like many other emerging markets, has a massive black market for goods and services. Smuggling is a popular profession in a country that borders so many that are faced with internal restrictions and lack of adequate supply chains. Turkey, because of its strategic location, is also a key player in the energy business—not from a production point of view, but rather as a location for major pipelines. Many of the countries around Turkey, especially Iran and Iraq, are major energy producers in the world.

Internally, more than 30 percent of the population is dependent on agriculture. Turkey is a regional breadbasket and the country has vast arable land. The country still faces major unemployment problems, as do most countries in Europe. More than 12 percent of the population is regarded as unemployed. This would be less of an issue were it not for the fact that the economy grew by more than 8 percent in 2010 and was on track for similar gains in 2011. With that kind of growth, job creation should be significant. It's not. Part of the problem is that Turkey's informal market leads to skewed statistics. Those who work for cash, and there are many hundreds of thousands who do, can at the same time bleed the government for benefits.

One of Turkey's greatest weaknesses of the past has been poor fiscal management. Tax collection is nearly impossible in a country where tax evasion is a pastime, something Turkey and Greece have in common. The government is always strapped for cash and this has led to massive deficit issues in the past and significant devaluation of its currency, the lira, to make up for its debtor status. The current government headed by Prime Minister Recep Erdogan has been in power since 2003 and is entering its third term. Under Erdogan, Turkey has deregulated the economy, privatized many state enterprises, and attracted foreign investment through a climate of economic certainty. The result has been 26 straight quarters of growth through 2011; foreign reserves of US$90 billion versus just over $20 billion in 1992; inflation of just under 6 percent, down from 40 percent a few years ago; and debt to GDP of less than 40 percent compared with 74 percent in 2002. Erdogan is a religious man who embraces his faith publicly, a rarity in Turkish politics. Yet, despite his constant efforts to push Turkey from its secular position and his friction with the military, he continues to receive strong popular support for his economic policies and his handling of Turkey's other problem.

The other problem is Turkey's constant struggle against the Kurdistan Workers' Party (PKK), a group that claims to represent the displaced Kurdish population. The Kurds have been seeking a separate state in what they consider their ancestral homeland in southeast Turkey and northern Iraq. They speak a different language, follow different customs, and have been involved in numerous attacks on military and civilian targets. In the past 25 years the conflict has resulted in more than 40,000 deaths, mainly on the Kurdish side. Erdogan has made strides (one of the requirements for entering the EU) in recognizing the Kurds through actions such as restoring Kurdish names to several towns, allowing Kurds to use their language in the local political arena, and trying to maintain good relations between the two ethnic groups. But, as recently as late 2011, Turkish planes bombarded Kurdish rebel strongholds in northern Iraq after insurgencies into Turkey by the PKK. This situation, while better than in the past, is still quite tenuous and could damage the country and presidency were it to escalate.

Local investment in Turkey should be restricted to Istanbul and the Turkish coast. These are the areas with greatest development potential for tourism, a huge money earner for Turkey. Real estate in Istanbul is not cheap unless you want to risk buying an apartment or house in the suburbs. Prices are high in comparison to other emerging markets and construction is not always of the best quality. However, the city continues to grow and tourism continues to increase. Real estate values have held up well throughout the ups and downs of the economy. Turkey has a fairly good-sized middle class, a rarity in the region. It does have its super rich oligarchs and its poor country peasants, but a good chunk of the population in Istanbul and in Ankara (the capital) enjoy a lifestyle comparable to that of countries that are on the verge of first-world status. The annual per capita income for Turks is more than $13,000, and using purchasing power metrics that equates to about $16,000, meaning that $13,000 in Turkey buys about $16,000 worth of goods and services in the United States.

Turkey is solidly a Tier 1 emerging market. This means that there is very little likelihood of it turning back economically. It has an established market system, good infrastructure, an established political system, and a population that is used to being relatively independent. While its secular status has been challenged in recent years, there is no indication that Turkey will not adhere to democratic principals regardless of who is in power. It is a country often overlooked by investors, yet it offers some of the best visibility in the region.

Strengths

Turkey boasts a secular democracy. It has strong military and economic ties to the United States and Europe. It occupies a strategic location in a very unstable region and has a strong and working capitalistic economic system. There is adequate transparency. It has a cosmopolitan population in major cities with a taste for Western consumption trends. Turkey enjoys a stable, popular government and strong economic growth and better-than-average fiscal discipline (currently). It is also a major tourist destination.

Weaknesses

Turkey's large black market inhibits adoption of a strong fiscal policy. It has lax tax collection and an overly large agrarian population that is not well educated or sophisticated. It has illiquid markets that are prone to volatility.

Opportunities

Turkey can show the rest of the Islamic world that success is achievable without strongman dictators or dependence on natural resources. It serves as a model for cooperation across religious and political boundaries. Tourism can be developed in the country's interior regions. It has the potential to become a first-world country through greater access to European markets and strengthening trade ties with the former Soviet bloc. Turkey is a resource hub with access to the Black Sea and the Mediterranean Sea.

Threats

There exists continued conflict with the Kurdish population. Turkey's current government is shifting to a more religious bent. The collapse of the European Union would impact Turkey negatively. There exists the threat of conflict with Greece over territorial rights, especially Cyprus. The lack of a strong tax collection system could force more government indebtedness. The strong military could oppose the current government attempt at moving to the right of center. Crises in other emerging markets could affect the country's efforts to attract Western and Eastern capital. When emerging markets get hit, Turkey is always affected negatively because of its past inability to deal with economic crises. If that happened today, Turkey would be a "strong buy."

Singapore

THE MODEL OF EFFICIENCY . . . AND SOMETIMES BOREDOM!

By far the richest country in Asia is Singapore. Of course, it's kind of like saying that Iceland was one of wealthiest country in Europe for a few months in the 2006 to 2009 period. Singapore is small, very small. Its population could fit in a small Chinese city, with room to spare. At just under five million people, including all the maids from the Philippines and Indonesia, the country barely registers on Asia's population map. But, through sound fiscal, monetary, economic, and social management Singapore has risen from a backwater 40 years ago to a country that has a greater income per capita than 90 percent of the world. One might argue that it is only possible in places with small, controllable populations, and one would probably be right.

You still can't buy chewing gum in Singapore, jaywalking will cost you a stiff fine, if you're caught spraying graffiti you will be caned, and if you are caught with narcotics you'll be put to death. If you can avoid those infractions and live with the stifling heat and humidity, Singapore is a good place to grab a couple of days of R&R on any Asian trip.

Where it shines though is as an investment destination. One would think that a country that has greater GDP and income per capita than most of the world, a AAA rating, a strong currency, a strong and transparent government, fiscal discipline, and a diverse but happy population, should have no place being an emerging market. Well, by virtue of its small size, location, and tendency to trade like its neighbors in boom and bust cycles, Singapore does belong in the category of emerging markets, albeit at the very top of the Tier 1 countries. If you look at the history of trading of the Singapore exchange, you can see where it suffers from massive sell-offs and massive surges in line with places like Indonesia, Thailand, Malaysia, and every other Asian emerging market.

Figure 8.1 shows you index values from late 1999 when the Stock Exchange of Singapore merged with the Singapore International Monetary Exchange to form the Singapore Exchange.

Now, these days, pretty much all charts look like this. Few exchanges globally are immune to crashes and bubbles. However, Singapore is different from non-emerging markets in that the exchange is dominated by a few companies and sectors. Of the total

Figure 8.1   Singapore Stock Market Index

market capitalization of approximately S$650 billion (US$387 billion), fully one-third is made up of companies in the financial and real estate sectors with another third coming from consumer goods and the services sector and less than one-seventh from the industrial sector. Singapore's business climate is geared toward finance, real estate, and services—all businesses that do extremely well during periods of high consumption and property booms but fade fast during periods of recession. It is not unusual for the Singapore market to have massive sell-offs due to the fact that such a few sectors can change the tide quickly. If you are looking to invest in Singapore, there are more than 770 companies that trade on the exchange . . . but if you're an American, you'll find it tough opening an account with a local Singaporean bank or broker without having to jump through a lot of hoops. You'll need to provide everything from a recent bank statement and passport to your most recent utility bill. They want to know who you are before they'll take your money, and they're not shy about saying no. But, it is possible for foreigners to invest in Singapore both directly and through exchange-traded funds and closed-end funds.

Singapore has to be timed in order for money to be made. That timing always coincides with booms and busts in the property markets. The top 30 companies make up an index called the Straits Times Index (STI). Much like the Dow 30 in the United States, the Straits Times is the benchmark most people look to in order to gauge the performance and health of the market.

Banks make up the three of the top four companies in the STI with SingTel, the Singaporean telecom giant, coming in third. The big news in Singapore recently is the introduction of casinos. On my recent trip in 2011, I visited the Marina Bay Sands property with its massive boat-shaped roofline overlooking the harbor. There is a nightclub at the top and an interesting restaurant called Ku De Ta, which attracts a lot of well-heeled foreigners and locals alike. It's not to be missed. The casino business in Singapore is second in the world only to that of Macau with Las Vegas coming in third, just to give you an idea of the impact of the business in Asia. Macau, the former Portuguese colony that was returned to China in 1999, dwarfs both Singapore and Vegas combined. You can buy into the casino business through a U.S. listed company, the Las Vegas Sands, which trades on the New York Stock Exchange under the symbol (NYSE:LVS). It also owns one of the biggest casinos in Macau. LVS is a great play on emerging market resort and gambling growth, but it does have a history of following Las Vegas and U.S. trends more closely than those in Asia.

For U.S. investors the IShares MSCI Singapore Index Fund is an excellent vehicle to provide diversified entry into Singapore. Of course, diversified in Singapore, as I mentioned earlier, means strong presences in banking, real estate, telecom, and travel and entertainment (including casinos). Table 8.1 lists the top holdings of the fund.

DBS, Oversea-Chinese, and United Overseas are top financials. Singapore Telecom is self explanatory as is Singapore Airlines. Genting is a large Malaysian conglomerate, and Genting Singapore is a casino holder. Keppel is an offshore marine, property, and infrastructure company. Wilmar is an agribusiness, Noble is a commodities trading company, and CapitaLand is involved in real estate development.

Table 8.2 shows the top holdings by sector.

There is one other Singapore listed company that I am a fan of. In fact, it was the focus of my most recent visit to Singapore in 2011.

Table 8.1   IShares MSCI Singapore Index Fund

Name	% of Fund
Dbs Group Holdings Ltd.	10.76
Singapore Telecom Ltd.	10.67
Oversea-Chinese Banking Corp.	9.77
United Overseas Bank Ltd.	9.45
Keppel Corp. Ltd.	6.39
Genting Singapore Plc.	4.61
Wilmar International Ltd.	4.42
Singapore Airlines Ltd.	3.27
Capitaland Ltd.	2.85
Noble Group Ltd.	2.81
Total	65.01

Source: http://us.ishares.com/product_info/fund/overview/
EWS.htm.

Table 8.2 Top Holdings by Sector

Sector	% of Fund
Financials	44.95
Industrials	25.55
Telecommunication services	11.32
Consumer discretionary	9.94
Consumer staples	7.73
S-T securities	0.02
Other/undefined	0.48
Total	100.00

Source: http://us.ishares.com/product_info/fund/overview/EWS.htm.

What's the most precious commodity on Earth? Hint: Despite the current furor over higher prices, it's not oil.

It's water. And drinkable water, of course, has only a finite supply—a big problem given that the global population (which last year topped seven billion people) is expected to grow by 40 to 50 percent over the next 50 years.

Fresh water demand exceeds supply by 17 percent. And demand is doubling every 21 years.

Serious shortages already exist in almost 100 countries. And the situation is particularly grave in the developing world.

In short, the world is running out of water.

And for all their emerging market prowess, regions like China, India, Latin America, and Africa are in particularly big trouble. Consider the following:

- China and India account for 40 percent of the world's population. Yet neither country has potable tap water. Two-thirds of China faces water shortages. And in big cities like New Delhi, groundwater is expected to dry up by 2015.
- In Latin America, about 15 percent of the population—76 million people—lacks safe water. And 116 million don't have sanitation services.
- Lack of safe water and sanitation costs the sub-Saharan region around 5 percent of its GDP each year.

So what's the answer? Well, there are increasingly innovative ways to make clean water from dirty water. And one company is doing just that in the most critical of regions.

Because of the massive profit potential that it holds, it's no wonder that analysts have dubbed the $460 billion global water market "blue gold."

But to scoop the biggest share, we need to dig a little deeper. For example, while large companies like General Electric and France's Veolia Environnement are major players, that's not going to get the job done for us.

Why? Because (1) neither company is a pure play on water, and (2) they aren't top-to-bottom providers, so there's a flaw in the business model.

Based in Singapore, Hyflux Ltd. (Pink Sheets:HYFXF) is a leading water industry player with a well-diversified focus on seawater desalination, water recycling and purification, wastewater treatment, and potable water treatment. Its desalination efforts are among the top three in the world.

Hyflux trumps its competition because it doesn't have to outsource its business. As a result, its margins are higher and it can outbid rivals on new projects, such as building new water plants. This key area of business has spawned a couple of profit streams.

For starters, it makes money from the initial design and construction of new plants, which takes about three years.

Hyflux also strategically partners with local authorities so that its projects make airtight financial sense. The partners provide some of the initial investment capital, but Hyflux runs the operations itself. And since the typical plant lifespan is 25 years, it earns 25 years' worth of returns.

But the best part?

Hyflux's target markets are China, India, the Middle East, and Southeast Asia. Those areas comprise more than 50 percent of the global market. Even better, they're growing and can afford to pay for clean water.

Over the next five years, for example, China is expected to spend close to half a trillion dollars on clean water. It simply has no choice.

Simply put, potable water is the single largest health problem in the world.

And more people = greater demand = shortages.

The above equation couldn't be simpler given that it includes two undeniable truths: The global population will keep growing, and there's a fixed amount of water on the planet.

The equation means a potentially massive payday, as the companies in the water business are in the early stages of a long period of prosperity.

Not only that, after meeting with Hyflux executives on my recent visit to Singapore, I believe that now is the best time to buy. For patient investors, the chance to hit this one out of the park is too compelling to pass up.

Singapore Girl

If you've never flown Singapore Airlines, it's a treat—until something goes wrong. "Singapore Girl" is one of the best-known ad campaigns for airline travel. Featuring perfectly coifed and manicured young flight attendants, the ads have been running since the 1970s and the flight attendants, who are as pretty in person, have become the iconic symbol for the airline. Singapore Airlines is known for its ultra modern fleet and in-flight amenities. I flew SIA on one of my trips to Singapore and it was almost everything advertised . . . until we took off from Taipei.

As a frequent traveler, I have been very lucky not to experience too many iffy flights or heavy turbulence—knock on wood. Taking off from Taipei, I was comfortably nestled in my upper deck seat on a Boeing 747 Megatop. The flight attendants, all Malaysian or Singaporean at the time, spoke perfect English and provided a level of service unsurpassed in my travels. About 15 minutes out of Taipei the plane shuddered. I noticed a flash of light outside my window. There was silence for what seemed to be an eternity. The flight attendants stopped speaking in English, adding to the feeling of unease in the cabin. The plane was still flying, so that was good news. After a few minutes the captain announced that one of the four engines had shut down. That was it. I noticed that for the next 60 minutes we were circling the same lights on the ground. It was impossible to talk to the attendants who were suddenly gathered in the galley and not being very social. In fact they looked quite scared. The captain then came on again and announced that we had almost completed dumping enough fuel so that we could land back in Taipei. I decided then that I would think twice about flying SIA, not because of some random engine explosion, but because of the lack of communication from the cockpit and the crew.

Things were decidedly better upon arrival in Singapore. A city-state, Singapore can easily be explored in a couple of days. In fact, if you have a layover of five hours or more there is a special program that allows for a city tour for passengers in transit (www.etour-singapore.com/free-singapore-tour.html). I have stayed at several hotels in the city, but my favorite to date is the Ritz-Carlton, Millenia with a beautiful view of the harbor and excellent service. If you are looking for a more nostalgic, but nonetheless excellent hotel, then choose the Raffles Hotel. It is the grande dame of Singapore and beautiful in its classical colonial design. The Singapore Sling was concocted by a Raffles bartender in 1915, although it sold for a lot less at the time than it does today. A Singapore Sling at the Long Bar will set you back a cool $25!

Singapore has two highlights in my opinion. Casinos you can enjoy anywhere and beaches as well. But what you will not find anywhere else is the variety of excellent foods available all over the city, especially in the open markets. It is one of the few countries where I will eat the street food, as health and cleanliness regulations are strictly enforced. In Singapore, you can get the best of Asian foods in one place. The population has a dominant mix of Malay, Chinese, and Indian. The cuisine is the best of all three and safe. Various neighborhoods offer local specialties and if there is one bargain in this expensive city, it is the food. One food in particular, durian, is very popular amongst Singaporeans. It's a fleshy fruit that comes in a weird-looking thorny husk that can vary in size, but is usually about the size of a melon. People here go wild over it—I am not among those people. The fruit has a distinctive odor, one that many who don't like it find quite offensive. Many places, like hotels, won't allow it to be consumed in indoor areas. To be honest it smells like dirty socks. But, it has a massive, deep-pocketed following with prices ranging from $4 to over $200 for rarer varieties. Buyer beware!

The second treat is the Night Safari. It's a fabulous experience to visit a zoological park at night and ride around in a tram while the nocturnal carnivores are feeding. If you've wanted to see a lion feeding ferociously on fresh meat, this is the place! You can find out more about the Night Safari at www.nightsafari.com.sg/. Be sure to bring mosquito repellant!

Shopping used to be the big draw in Singapore in the 1980s and 1990s, especially for electronics as the country was a major thoroughfare in Asia as well as a manufacturer. The duty-free zone in Singapore Changi Airport is likely the largest in the world, bigger than most shopping malls in the United States. But today, prices are quite expensive and not really competitive with prices online or even at box stores in the United States. The selection is outrageous, though. Clothing is still quite reasonable, and Singaporeans love to shop about as much as they like to eat. Singapore has come a long way in the past 45 years from a backwater port where the per capita income in 1965 was less than US$700 per year to the wealthiest city in Asia today with annual per capita income of over US$44,000 and growing. Unfortunately, the country has become a little too expensive and reliant on buoyancy from ultra high real estate prices and its booming financial center. In the event of an Asian downturn, Singapore will survive but could suffer significantly more than it would appear from surface observations.

Strengths

Singapore has a strong, transparent financial system and strong laws governing the day-to-day life of its residents. It has a superb infrastructure and a natural port and harbor with a long history of commerce. Singapore is one of Asia's major financial centers on par with the likes of Hong Kong. And the country has a strong multicultural consumption-based economy.

Weaknesses

Singapore has a heavy reliance on a few sectors for growth, namely real estate, finance, and tourism as well as a strong reliance on foreign workers due to its very small indigenous domestic workforce. Its laws are heavy-handed and prohibit some personal freedoms for the sake of the greater good of the people. It is a small country with its own currency that could be subject to stronger macro shocks.

Opportunities

It could become the non-Sino hub for Asian commerce. Its reputation as a private banking sector with strict privacy laws will continue to attract capital—it is the Switzerland of Asia in this regard, although it is slowly succumbing to less stringent privacy laws, as is the rest of the world.

Threats

The country's over-reliance on foreign labor is beginning to make Singaporeans fat and happy and taking away some of the drive that made the country what it is. It is expensive. The country is beginning to out-price itself and taking on more of a Monaco-like status for Asia. This could lead to social unrest among the low-paid imported working class, something that would be put down harshly by a government not afraid to use force to maintain the appearance of harmony. A strong global assault on banking privacy could undermine the country's status as a tax haven and a center for private banking.

9

Russia and the CIS

PAINFUL PROSPERITY—REINVENTING A SOCIETY

I knew that I would be in for a wild ride when I boarded my first Aeroflot flight. The plane was decrepit to put it kindly, with seatbelts that were torn. The pilots, former military flyers, taxied down the runway, and before I knew it I was looking straight up as the jet went vertical until we reach cruising altitude. Flight attendants dressed in what looked like nurse uniforms walked down the aisles handing out apple juice from rickety carts. It was 1982.

Russian language was one of my minors in college and I was fortunate to have been taught by two dedicated professors: Edward Danowitz, who taught the Apollo astronauts basic Russian for their meeting in space with their Soyuz counterparts; and Sasha Boguslavski, who led my first trip to the former Soviet Union. In retrospect, as enjoyable as Russian was, I should have studied Chinese!

I was fortunate to first visit Russia when it was still in the throes of communist rule. Yuri Andropov, the premier, had just died. I knew that, it was all over the news. But, the majority of Russians and Soviets had no idea. They were told he was ill. And, like a nation spoon-fed everything else, they believed it.

By the time I returned home after more than a month, I had lost 15 pounds. The only other country where I can lose weight so fast is China. My diet consisted of Tuc crackers and Fanta or Pepsi

Cola. There was little to eat that was appetizing unless borscht is up your alley or some strange fish covered in a layer of jelly. We could buy bread at Bread Store Number 7 down the street from the Pribaltiyskaya Hotel or some bruised apples if they were available. Once in a while, we'd be treated to some shashlik—shish kabobs—but even they were gristly and mostly inedible. I was so hungry one night that I went to the best hotel in Moscow at the time, the Metropol Hotel, thinking I could get some real food. You must remember that at the time the ruble was basically worthless against the U.S. dollar and everything was cheap. I looked at the menu and ordered a whole chicken. It arrived promptly. I have never seen a chicken that had no meat on it until that night! It was back to my hotel for some cheap but filling *beli hleb* (white bread).

Moscow, St. Petersburg, and Kiev (in Ukraine) are spectacular cities. Their wide avenues were so well lit at the time that taxicabs would leave their lights off at night. The architecture with the gilded onion domes of the Kremlin and the museums like the Pushkin and the Hermitage were beyond compare—a little shabby but spectacular, nonetheless. Everyone had a job. Elderly women—babushkas—were sweeping the streets, veterans wearing all their war medals manned the coat checks everywhere we went. The country was poor, but it was functioning and the government's welfare state was in full swing.

On each floor in the hotel there was a matronly character sitting in front of a desk opposite the elevator 24 hours a day to make sure we were not bringing contraband, human or otherwise, to our rooms. They would also make us hot tea whenever we wanted it. Drinking water was not potable and tea was the best option to avoid getting sick. Getting sick was quite easy. Some of my fellow travelers experienced this firsthand when they drank the water a few hours prior to taking an overnight train from Moscow to St. Petersburg in the dead of winter. While we slept in cozy bunks, they spent the night sitting on splintered wooden toilet seats buffeted by subzero temperatures. I always wonder why people don't take the simplest precautions when traveling.

St. Petersburg is a beautiful city, one of the most beautiful I have ever seen. Nevsky Prospekt is one of the grandest streets in the world, lined with nightclubs, restaurants, and shops. It's the main thoroughfare in the city. What struck me most about St. Petersburg, and the Soviet Union in general, was the unbelievably beautiful architecture and statuary to be found everywhere. It was a testament to both the love of arts of the former tsars and tsarinas, and also a reminder of the days of oppression and serfdom that led to the Bolshevik Revolution. The masses were better off in 1982, but sadness was the order of the day.

As Westerners we stuck out like sore thumbs. It was hard not to. We wore clothes with colors that weren't gray, seemingly the national color. It seemed that somberness was celebrated and happiness a rare commodity. The prevailing mood stood in sharp contrast to the background. Imagine traveling down hundreds of feet on an escalator to a subway platform so deep in the ground that it was doubtless designed to be a bomb shelter. On the platform you were surrounded by artwork and massive ornate chandeliers—a testament to the wealth accumulated by the country. But all around you were silent, gray ghosts resigned to a life of melancholic anonymity. They were prisoners of their own making, living life ignorant of what was occurring in the outside world. If they stepped out of line, they faced harsh punishment. Visitors often commented on the number of bread trucks they saw on the streets of a country where food was scarce only later to find out that many of the trucks were used to transport dissidents and others that the ever-present Big Brother wanted to silence or send to the Gulags.

People were scared. Everyone whispered so as not to attract attention either from the plain-clothed KGB fops or from listening devices. At a party in our room, our guests pointed immediately to the ceilings as the preferred place for listening devices. When I stood at the airport in Minsk, Belarus, taking photos, my camera was stripped from my hands and the film removed. The airport was also a military air base. If I were not a tourist, I would have certainly fared much worse.

Propaganda was the order of the day. The secondary purpose of the trip was for a group of us to do interviews with members of the Russian television media about a book that we worked on called the *Best of Pravda*, a compilation of translations of the politically charged anti-Western cartoons that appeared daily in the major newspaper, *Pravda*. Pravda in Russian means "truth." We joked that there was little truth in *Pravda*. During the interviews we invariably talked about the lack of free speech, the views of dissident author

Alexander Solzhenitsyn, and the overall perverse view of the West that the Russians held. None of it ever appeared on the program when it aired.

When we weren't interacting with the media we spent time shopping. There was nothing to buy in the stores, of course. The big shopping center, GUM (goom), was replete with shops carrying nothing but poor-quality clothing. But on the streets and in the back alleys there was a treasure trove to be bought, and bought cheaply. The U.S. dollar was king and the exchange rate on the street, if you didn't get ripped off first, was three times that of the official rate. We bought everything from beautiful Russian lacquer works to fur coats, fur hats, balalaikas, chess sets, you name it. Often we didn't use cash, but traded blue jeans (we knew ahead of time to bring several pairs) and packs of Marlboro Reds. I even traded a reversible belt for a beautiful lacquer box with a troika painted on it—one of my prized memories from the trip. Since the belt was reversible, I got my counterpart to throw in a fur hat as well! The biggest problem was getting everything out of the country. The Soviets did not turn a blind eye to anything. Fortunately, airport pat downs were rare back then and some of us strapped the wares to our bodies—it was winter and bulky was the fashion!

Out of the Frying Pan and into the Fire

The former Soviet Union came into being in 1991. After a period of liberal thinking prodded by Mikhail Gorbachev, the official dissolution was orchestrated by Boris Yeltsin in 1991. Unlike popular revolutions like the one that led to the formation of the Soviet Union, this revolution was created by the state apparatus out of desperation. The Soviet Union had to break up or Russia, the biggest country, would not survive. It was a financial decision and a tacit admission that 74 years of communism was a failure beyond measure. It caught the people off guard completely, and to this day a vast majority of the population in places like Russia, Ukraine, and Belarus pine for the days of communist rule—not because they enjoyed the lack of freedom, but because they knew the certainty of a welfare state where everything was provided for them, albeit sparsely. Health care was free, pensions were worth something, jobs were created, food was on the table, housing was cheap, and excellent educations were attainable by the masses. There was only one problem. And the problem could not be foreseen by a population that was ill prepared for a seismic shift in its way of life. The problem was that the state was broke: massive military overspending, little in the way of surplus capital, obsolete factories, massive public debt burdens, and a population that produced little in the way of exportable goods for hard, valuable currency. Add to this massive corruption at municipal, state, and federal levels and the recipe for failure was mixed many decades ago.

For the average Russian, Ukrainian, Kazakh, Uzbek, or Lithuanian there was only one truth: No country in the world was more powerful, richer, and fairer than the U.S.S.R. They learned the hard way that nothing they had heard or read for decades was true. In fact, aside from a strong military, the U.S.S.R. was nothing but a ragtag collection of republics that, for the most part, did not get along with each other prior to the formation of the union, and all of which learned to hate Russia the most after the collapse.

Each country was on its own. Each had to develop new governments, new currencies, new social institutions, new trade agreements, new everything. Today the result of the collapse is still being felt in many parts of the former U.S.S.R. Pensioners beg for food, health care is outrageously expensive as is decent food and clothing. Energy costs are extremely high, and threats of shortages due to unpaid bills to the producers are common. The only thing that remains the same is corruption, and that has been taken to new heights.

Today, the former republics of the U.S.S.R. are firmly entrenched in the second and even the third tier of emerging market status. The rule of law in places like Russia can change overnight. Overt strong-arm tactics once practiced by the government are now covert tactics practiced by former members of the KGB, who have basically usurped power. In poorer Republics, despots have taken over power and control vast resources of oil and other commodities. In the Baltics, efforts at European-style commercial activity and government are perhaps the only shining light left from the shell of what was once considered a massive and powerful empire.

It's not an easy task to invest in the former Soviet Union. There are a few options, however. And, as with any emerging market, the options are very volatile and, for the most part, investing in the former Soviet Union is perhaps best reserved for professionals and not for individual investors. So mutual funds and exchange-traded funds are the rule. It's best to break the region into three categories: the Russian bloc of Russia, Ukraine, Belarus, Moldova, and Georgia; the Baltic bloc of Lithuania, Latvia, and Estonia; and the Asian bloc comprising Kazakhstan, Uzbekistan, Turkmenistan, Kyrgyzstan, Tajikistan, Azerbaijan, and Armenia.

Beneath the Amber Curtain

My first investment in Russia was a parking garage in Moscow in the mid-1990s. It turned out to be a bust. Not because the garage was not successful but because it was impossible to track the investment and property rights were fuzzy at best. My next investment was through two highly volatile investments. One was the closed-end Templeton Russia Fund and the second was in a cellular company called Vimpelcom. I invested in both after the Russian financial crisis, which began in late 1997, triggered by the collapse in the Asian markets earlier in the year. They were both excellent trades as I recall and set the stage for future trades in Russian equities, all of which were made during times of crisis.

If you're going to invest in Russia, go small and wait for the inevitable crises that occur with regularity. There is nothing kosher about stocks or companies in the region. All are subject to the whim of government meddling. The place is corrupt from the top down, and knowing this fact makes Russia the worst of the BRIC (Brazil, Russia, India, and China) countries as far as transparency goes.

Let's step back for a minute and look at the structure of the Russian and Ukrainian story. The other countries, Belarus, Moldova, and Georgia are not worth spending much ink on, as they are barely economically viable countries.

When Yeltsin took power Russia was an economic mess. Huge debts—internal and external—a crumbling currency, obsolete factories, overemployment, and massive inefficiency and corruption were the rule of the day. Some businessmen were making money though by smuggling goods into Russia—things like computers, blue jeans, and cigarettes were in huge demand. They were able to sell their wares because of their connections to the power brokers in the Russian government, who took a healthy cut of the profits to look the other way.

As a cornerstone of the transition from state-run enterprises to privately held businesses, Yeltsin and his advisors embarked on a course to privatize Russian state-owned enterprises. To understand the scope of this, think about *all* the companies in the United States—from trash collection to steel mills to bakeries—being owned by the U.S. government and then *given* to the public at large. Prior to this time it was illegal to own a business in Russia.

The intention was right but the results were disastrous for the vast majority of the population. Vouchers were distributed to everyone, including minors. But the masses did not understand what was going on as they had no idea what a nongovernment-run or -owned business was. Most quickly surrendered their vouchers to the management of these businesses for something they did not have: cash. These managers and the few black marketers who had money bought everything on the cheap, thereby shutting out almost the entire population from future benefits of the businesses. Much of the non-black-market money came directly through the Russian governmental connections. In effect, what happened was the very government officials who privatized the companies ended up owning these companies for themselves, their cronies, and their friends.

What ensued was concentrated ownership of the entire complex of businesses by a small group of individuals who came to be known as the oligarchs. What the oligarchs knew was that their new businesses would have support from the government, as they were still the biggest spenders on goods and services. In return for this bargain, the oligarchs would pad the coffers of individual government officials for decades to come. If they didn't, the government officials would use their enforcement mechanisms to either jail, kill, or confiscate the wealth from the oligarchs at will. This process repeated itself in the other Commonwealth of Independent States countries, as the former republics were called, with varying results.

The Khodorkovsky Case

Mikhail Khodorkovsky was the CEO and major shareholder of Yukos, a large Russian oil company. At one time he was the richest man in Russia, worth billions. Without a doubt, this oligarch benefited from the voucher program. However, he did something different. Instead of managing the firm with secrecy regarding its books and records, he embraced transparency, brought in Western board members, and pushed for more openness in Russian business. This put him at odds with the government and especially Vladimir Putin, then the Russian president and currently prime minister, and maybe soon-to-be president again. Putin, a former cook for Joseph Stalin, made his way up the ranks and was installed as leader of the FSB—the new KGB—by Yelstin. That set the stage for his rise to power over Russia in the years post Yeltsin. He was a reformer and introduced many economic reforms, however, he was less of a reformer when it came to politics and governance. He is a strong believer in more government and less individual freedom.

Khodorkovsky crossed the line with his actions and his outspoken criticism of the government. In October 2003, he was negotiating to sell a stake in Yukos to a major U.S. oil company when he was suddenly arrested and thrown in jail. The charges ranged from corruption to tax evasion. The result was that the richest man in Russia, who many thought was protected by his wealth and power, was now in Siberia, serving time. He still sits in jail today after numerous failed appeals. Yukos is now, once again, controlled by the government through its state-owned oil company, Rosneft, which claims to own Yukos debt. After the Khodorkovsky incident, many oligarchs, who once thought themselves untouchable, fled Russia or developed an even closer friendship to the Kremlin.

The Yukos incident spells out the risk of investing in Russia. What is private one day could be state-owned the next day. As an investor, that is a huge risk to take and a good reason why investing in Russia should be done only with pure risk capital—the type you can afford to lose in a worst-case scenario.

But, the flipside is that Russia will always present opportunities for trading, as the governmental antics are not going to stop. The country is a huge oil producer and rich in natural resources. While oil prices remain at elevated levels, the government and the oligarchs will continue to enjoy the fruits of their ownership of those resources.

The people on the street, on the other hand, are living a life of dismal hardship. The government could not care less about individuals or individual freedom. It is the power, controlling business, the military, and the legislative process with an iron fist. It is a country on a collision course with anarchy, once again.

The Baltics

The Baltic countries of Latvia, Lithuania, and Estonia have never identified with their former Russian overlords. They shared neither language nor culture with them. More European (Germanic/Nordic) in descent than Slavic, the Baltics were forced to embrace Russia and the Russian language, but only by military threat and occupation. You would be hard pressed to find a single non-Russian individual who harbored anything but resentment toward the former Soviet Union.

I knew from the moment I set foot in Tallinn, the capital of Estonia, that it was a different place completely from any of the Soviet cities I had visited. The people were friendlier, the buildings more colorful, and the food was actually edible. It was the first time on my trip, after almost three weeks of the worst food I had ever eaten, that I actually enjoyed a meal. I remember it vividly—chicken breast and French fries . . . I think I ate three servings!

The three countries are part of the European Union with Estonia adopting the euro currency in 2011. The other two will follow in the coming years. While fast growing, the economies are quite small as are the populations, which when combined would be fewer than that of the New York metropolitan area.

What the Baltics offer, as my friend Kevin Kerr, a successful commodities trader who resides there part of the year, has discovered, is a great standard of living for those who earn Western salaries but spend in Eastern countries. The countries sport slightly higher per capita income relative to their Russian and Asian counterparts, averaging just over $10,500 per year. The relatively low cost of living and strong European feel of the countries and especially their capitals, Tallinn, Riga, and Vilnius, make for an interesting second or primary home proposition—especially for those seeking backdoor entry into the EU.

The Asian Republics

These former Soviet republics border Russia to the south. They have more in common culturally with countries like Turkey than those of their former brethren to the north. I remember vividly standing in an elevator of a Moscow hotel when an Uzbek walked in. I felt as one might have felt in the old American South when segregation was in effect. The cultures clash in every possible way. But, these republics are rich in natural resources, especially places like Kazakhstan. Few people realize that Kazakhstan is a real place and not some made up place from a Borat movie. Boasting the largest reserves of oil in the Caspian Sea region, Kazakhstan is the size of Western Europe—it's massive.

However, one other similarity that is shared by most of these pseudo Asian countries is that they are ruled by a cadre of benevolent dictators with relatively low levels of freedom for the people and relatively poor distribution of wealth. Most of the countries are Islamic nations, as well, which has allowed for expanded ties to the countries to the south like Turkey and Iran.

The only real investment opportunities here are in the oil/gas/resource sector. But, my experience has been that most of the companies, and a couple have listed on U.S. and London exchanges, have been pretty sketchy. News releases are often short and not timely and there are significant credibility issues when dealing with countries that are small and ruled by pseudo dictatorial regimes, which are more tribal and familial. They operate much like the oligarchies of Russia and Ukraine.

Strengths

The region has massive natural resources. Russia produces more oil daily than Saudi Arabia, but its reserves are a third of those in Saudi. The Baltics allow for easier entry into the European Union with an educated, low-cost workforce and less corrupt parliamentary democracies.

Russia has a strong military force and there is a vast infrastructure developed in the Soviet times as well as extensive port systems.

Weaknesses

It is difficult to invest in the former Soviet republics. There are ETFs and country funds like the Templeton Russia Fund (NYSE:TRF) and a host of mutual and hedge funds, as well. A former intern and colleague of mine runs a fund for Firebird Management (www.fbird.com/). They have extensive experience in investing in the region and have proved to be quite resilient. But as is the case with any other fund or investor, money is only made in Russia and the region during boom periods and can easily be lost overnight. It's not for the faint of heart. Other problems include currency controls, a lack of transparency in accounting and government, and poor social safety nets; they are nonexistent in many of the countries. The Russian bloc has high rates of alcoholism. There is little spending on infrastructure other than for natural resource pipelines.

Opportunities

This is not China, India, or Brazil. Russia is fraught with risks beyond those of economic cycles. Opportunities are available in the natural resource sector in the Asian countries, but contracts are very hard to enforce. The Baltic bloc offers great opportunities for expatriation if the climate is not an issue.

Threats

There is a huge divide between the mega rich and the poor. Oligarchs and government operatives in the Russian bloc thrive on chaos. There is a Russian mafia, which has close ties to the government. Asian countries have poor popular representation and are prone to violent coups in the future. Russia itself could face major political, popular, and economic issues in the future as the poorest in the society, an educated mass, reach the point of desperation. As a nuclear superpower, Russia will always possess a bigger bark than bite, impeding global progress in the

Middle East and Asia where Russia holds significant commercial interests.

Russia and the former Soviet republics have never recovered from the collapse of the U.S.S.R. There are questions about rule of law, distribution of equity, and transparency of markets. Until those are resolved, the region, minus the Baltics, will face significant problems for years, if not decades, to come. Unless you are an adept trader with a high tolerance for risk, the region is not a place that I would recommend for investment.

CHAPTER 10

Brazil

THE GIRL FROM IPANEMA . . .
GOT CARJACKED!

Brazil. What comes to mind is Rio, Copacabana, the statue of Christ the Redeemer on Corcovado Hill, Carnaval. What comes to mind is a vibrant population that seems to revel in the joy of life. Then, I talk to people who have been to Brazil. The country is booming, but massive social problems still prevail. Residents of Rio worry more about being kidnapped or carjacked then they do about the economic miracle. That is the reality on the ground.

The largest country both in terms of land area and population in South America, it has become the economic miracle of this century. Rich in natural resources, the country has been a favorite of emerging markets investors for the past two decades. But the sailing has been far from smooth in this economy prone to massive booms, busts, and hyperinflation. But, the country seems to have turned a corner, and done so under a socialist president, something few thought would happen. In the 1980s and early 1990s, Brazil saw rates in excess of 300 percent annual inflation.

When Luiz Inacio Lula da Silva took power in the 2002 election, people around the world were stunned. He had run twice before, unsuccessfully. He was seen by many as ultra-left politically, someone who clawed his way through factory jobs, someone with little formal education, and someone who made his name organizing labor unions. He was once jailed for a month, charged with organizing labor rallies in the 1970s, a time when Brazil was under military rule. By the time he left office in 2010, Lula was hailed as the most popular politician in Brazil's history.

His policies and progressive thinking strengthened the country's currency, opened the floodgates for economic growth and energy independence, and brought a sense of pride to a country that had lost its way in the 1990s.

In 2001, Argentina, Brazil's neighbor, defaulted on its foreign debt to the International Monetary Fund (IMF), which bailed the country out of economic crisis in the 1990s. Brazil, on the other hand, which had been the largest emerging market IMF debtor nation up to that point, paid off its debt to the IMF in full in 2005. In 2008, Brazil became a creditor nation—one that is owed more than it owes, a stunning reversal. Partly in recognition of its progress, Brazil was awarded the 2016 Summer Olympic Games, a first for a South American country.

Lula's plan was to implement his policies of investing money in education, social programs, pension reform, and welfare for the poor and working class. Focus on exports has led this resource-rich country into the twenty-first century at the top of the list of Tier 1 emerging markets. But, while on the surface everything appears rosy, a look below reveals issues that may derail economic expansion and may even lead the country into recession in the years ahead.

Lula's plan for Brazil's recovery was implemented through heavy government spending and, while that allowed millions of families to rise out of poverty, the country's recovery also owed much to its strong export sector, a sector very dependent on commodities prices and the commodities boom that has prevailed for much of the past decade. As that boom fades or as global economies slow, Brazil will face lower export revenue at a time when government spending is on the rise. Skyscrapers are popping up everywhere, money is being spent for the upcoming Olympics, but the country still suffers from inadequate tax revenue, a low savings rate, and massive poverty outside the biggest cities. Inflation is starting to rise again on the back of a 10-year boom, and interest rates are rising in an effort to cool growth. The higher rates and economic growth are attracting lots of short-term capital playing the risk trade, borrowing in dollars and investing in reals. The Brazilian real has been on a rollercoaster ride, trading as high as

1.64 to the dollar in 2013. Today the real is trading at close to 4 to the dollar, a massive devaluation that has put additional pressure on the economy. Brazilians are spending less overseas, but the export sector should benefit from the weak currency.

Brazil is now a Tier 1 emerging market, however, last year a major battle broke out in one of Rio's slums, something akin to a war. The military was called in and by the end of the skirmish, more that 42 lay dead. Events like this are not uncommon in emerging markets that suffer from massive economic inequality. Socially, it still suffers from instability beneath the surface that could lead to government heavy handedness. But, there is little doubt that Brazil will ever revert to a military dictatorship or hyperinflation. More likely, the country will suffer lower growth than the current 8 percent as world economies cool and commodities demand falters. But, growth in other emerging markets and the continued long-term trend in commodity prices bode very well for the country's long-term outlook. In 2008/2009 Brazil saw economic contraction as the world suffered from the recession in the United States. However, growth in this emerging market was the first to rebound, a testament to its resiliency compared to days past.

Few people realize that Brazil is a major player in several world markets. It produces more than 80 percent of the orange juice consumed worldwide. It has the largest cattle population of any country in the world. It has huge oil reserves and is a net exporter of oil. It is also a major producer of sugar cane and coffee. Brazil's problem has never been that it was not rich, rather that the wealth was concentrated amongst a very small upper class. This inequality continues today, but as I mentioned earlier, the Lula government took steps that are directly benefiting the lower classes, such as increasing the minimum wage and reforming the pension system.

Brazil is a major trader on the world market and especially in the South American region. The country is almost as big in size as the United States and borders every country in South America, save Chile and Ecuador. It is home to the world's largest rainforest and the biggest river (the Amazon is nearly twice the size of the Nile although it is slightly shorter in length). Its biggest trading partner is actually not in the Americas; it is China. China's need for natural resources plays into the hands of the Brazilian economy and that should be a trend that continues for many years to come.

Infrastructure in Brazil is quite impressive, as well. The country has more than one million miles of roadways (paved and unpaved) putting it behind only the United States, China, and India and well ahead of any European nation and Russia. The country also has the second highest number of airports in the world, albeit the majority are landing strips. It's a country well equipped to lead growth in the Americas for many years to come as long as it can refrain from fiscal irresponsibility, which has plagued its past.

Investor Friendly . . . to a Point

Investing in Brazil is quite easy. Unlike in many emerging markets, there is plenty to choose from depending on your tastes. The three most popular investment classes in the country are banks, oil, and natural resources. All three are quite volatile and can provide extremely good returns if you can time your investment. The Bovespa is the main stock exchange in Brazil, located in Sao Paulo, the country's financial capital. It's a major world exchange with a market capitalization exceeding US$1.5 trillion.

There are dozens of companies that trade as American depositary receipts (ADR) on U.S. exchanges such as the NYSE and NASDAQ. You can get a full list of ADRs for any country on this site: www.adr.com.

The two most popular companies for investment in Brazil are oil giant Petrobras (PBR:NYSE) and Vale SA (VALE:NASDAQ), the mining giant. Petrobras is South America's largest company by market capitalization and sales, and by far the largest company in Brazil. Vale is the second largest company in Brazil. The two combined tend to drive the Bovespa's price movement on any given day. This is an important point to note if you are considering investing in Brazil through an exchange-traded fund like the Ishares Brazil (EWZ:NYSE) or through a closed-end fund like the Brazil Real Fund (BZF:NYSE), which trades the currency. EWZ's two largest components are Petrobras and Vale, which make up close to 30 percent of the holdings, leading to more than average volatility because of narrow concentration. The Brazil Real Fund, managed by Wisdom Tree (www.wisdomtree.com/etfs/fund-details-currency.asp?etfid=63), gives you the ability to diversify your currency into the Brazilian

real, which has returned over 36 percent since the fund's inception in 2008 as the real has steadily appreciated against the U.S.
dollar.

If you're looking for alternative investment classes consider
Banco Bradesco (BBD:NYSE), one of Brazil's largest private banks,
with a huge retail presence. With interest rates over 10 percent in
Brazil, the banking sector has been able to attract a ton of foreign
investment and inflows allowing it to lend robustly. However, as we
have seen in the United States, banks are not the smartest lenders
in the world. Banco Bradesco shares tend to outperform U.S. counterparts in the good times, but fall as hard, or even harder, when
corrections occur.

Other options for investing in Brazil that are attractive are companies in the home-building sector like Gafisa (GFA:NYSE) and
Rossi Residential.

Resource Is King

Brazil's two largest companies, Petrobras and Vale, are world players.
Petrobras is a semiprivate company controlled by the government
and also by shareholders. It is hugely profitable and an aggressive
explorer in many countries, but particularly off the coast of Brazil.
The company is one of the technological leaders when it comes
to exploration because it dares to drill deeper than any other
company. One of the company's former petroleum geologists,
Dr. Marcio Mello, and I have met several times. He has presented
extensively about his work in the private sector as president of
HRT Petroleum, an exploration company based in Rio. But, what
intrigued me the most about our conversations was what he has
to say about Petrobras, his former company . . . and when he said
it. Our first meeting was at a conference a few years back when he
was explaining to a stunned audience about how Petrobras' drilling technology has taken it to depths of almost 23,000 feet (80 percent of the height of Mt. Everest) below the ocean's subsalt surface,
the layer well below the ocean's surface. Estimates range from
30 billion to as many as 70 billion barrels of oil in this part of the
subocean surface. The higher-end estimates would put the finds on
par with those of the North Sea fields off the coasts of the United
Kingdom and Norway.

However, Petrobras can be viewed as nothing but a very long term speculation at this point. The depth of corruption and graft has led to the door of the President's office. Brazilian president Dilma Rousseff was part of the Board of Directors of Petrobras during the period of time of the corruption allegations and she also served as Minister of Energy during the tenure of her predecessor, Luiz Inacio Lula da Silva, popularly known as "Lula".

The share price has been decimated as a result of the scandal and the huge debt load the company carries. It is the quintessential example of investing in emerging markets—nothing is as it appears on the surface. I view Petrobras as a long term option on both Brazil and oil prices. Its chances of surviving and prospering are as good as its chances of being nationalized or broken up. It is not for the faint of heart.

Oil prices are under pressure on several fronts. The biggest threat comes from the continued overproduction by Saudi Arabia and the members of the OPEC cartel. Oil markets crashed in 2014-2015 as the Saudis went "nuclear" to try to head off the threat form US shale producers, which ramped up production in the United States to the highest levels since the 1970s and catapulted the country into the top spot for total energy production.

As a result, the world is awash in oil and natural gas, leading to immense pressure on countries like Brazil that are geared towards exporting oil and other commodities. One of the world's biggest growing consumers is China, and the Chinese are experiencing a slowdown from the heady days of 10 percent annual GDP growth to a more moderate pace in the mid-single digits. However, the future for consumption from places like China and India continues to look bright as both economies are still in expansion mode.

China, which will surpass the United States in total oil consumption this decade, still lags in per capita consumption, as do all emerging countries. Table 10.1 offers a selected look at world oil consumption. (Please see the Appendix for a complete oil consumption chart.)

The oil consumption chart from 2010 shows that China's oil consumption is 9.18 million barrels per day, while the United States consumes over 19 million barrels per day and India comes in at just over 3 million barrels per day. As the chart clearly shows, a huge gap oil consumption exists globally. With China and India growing in the mid to high single digits and massive numbers of middle class oil consumers being added daily, the future for oil looks very

**Table 10.1   Selected World Oil Consumption
Rankings (barrels per day—2010)**

World Rank	Country	Barrels per Day
1	United States	19,150,000
2	European Union	13,730,000
3	China	9,189,000
5	India	3,182,000
6	Russia	2,937,000
7	Brazil	2,654,000
12	Mexico	2,073,000
18	Indonesia	1,292,000
19	Singapore	1,080,000
22	Thailand	988,000
25	Egypt	740,000
27	Turkey	646,300
29	Argentina	618,000
30	Poland	564,500
31	Malaysia	561,000
32	South Africa	553,000
34	Pakistan	410,000
38	Hong Kong	333,000
39	Vietnam	320,000
41	Philippines	310,000
42	Chile	302,700
44	Ukraine	296,000
116	Nicaragua	30,000

Source: www.cia.gov/library/publications/the-world-factbook/
rankorder/2174rank.html.

bright. And oil companies like Petrobras will continue to be major players for a long time to come. The only question is whether it will emerge from the scandal and remain a public company...and therein lies the risk.

During oil price sell-offs, which occur with regularity and during emerging market sell-offs, companies like those in Brazil experience corrections that are more magnified than they should be considering the long-term potential. That is the fun in investing, as far as I am concerned. It is the opportunity to make money when others are selling because of fear or panic. You have to take advantage of these pricing opportunities to trade and accumulate shares in these companies. The emerging markets correction offers investors a rare occasion to accumulate emerging markets shares on the cheap. Resource companies like Brazil's Vale are here to stay and will flourish as the world's demand for commodities grows.

Sure, there is a lot of talk about alternative energy and that is the long-term path that we all must follow. But, consider this. Based on current trends in alternative energy, sources of non-fossil-fuel consumption worldwide make up about 10 percent of energy consumed today and in the best possible case will make up 20 percent or thereabouts in 20 years from now based on studies put forth by various proponents of alternative fuel consumption. The price of oil will have quite a bit to do with how this alternative energy cycle pans out. If oil prices decrease, it will take longer to switch as there is less incentive, especially among emerging market nations that care more about growth than they do about pollution or renewable energy.

The Sweet Spot in Resources

Vale (VALE:NASDAQ) is by far the largest mining company in South America and one of the top five in the world. Vale is also the largest producer in the world of iron ore pellets and the second largest miner of nickel.

This and other mining activities puts Vale in the commodities sweet spot vis-à-vis China and other Asian emerging markets as what it mines is necessary for construction, especially steel for buildings and infrastructure. One major issue, one that Vale has overcome so far by being a lower cost producer, is proximity to China and status as a ship-borne miner. Its biggest market is much easier to reach by the major Australian miners that are the company's largest competitors in the iron ore business.

Vale was a state-owned "public" enterprise until 1997 when it was privatized by the government. In 2006 the company acquired Canada's second largest mining company, Inco, a major nickel miner, for a staggering US$19 billion, $17.7 billion of which was paid in cash. This made headlines because it made Vale number two in nickel behind Russian miner Norilsk and also because it was the largest acquisition ever made by a Brazilian company.

Vale was a hugely profitable company during the commodities boom of the last decade. China was booming and their appetite for iron ore and other resources was insatiable. That era is over and companies like Vale have suffered as a result. But, the company is restructuring to meet a lower demand model that looks to last for a few more years. It still represents an excellent value at current levels, both as a play on Brazil and for a play on the commodities sector when it eventually recovers.

If there is a common thread for most of these emerging markets stories, it is Chinese and Asian demand. Almost every mining company in South America and Australia has profited on the back of Asia and looks to that region and nowhere else for growth.

But China is slowing, and while other parts of Asia will pick up some slack, India in particular, it is China that holds the key for mega-growth going forward. If the cycle of growth has indeed turned, then countries like Brazil will have to endure a recessionary period before any recovery can take place. Mines will have to close, drilling for oil will have to slow, and government overhaul will become a necessity, not an option. The days of 6 percent growth and a strong consumer sector will not be revisited for years.

However, if Brazil can get its act together and show that it can survive both an economic, political, and commodities bust, then the current timing may prove to be ideal for investors looking for a beaten down emerging market that does have potential. Companies like Vale are the types of companies you can pick up for the low single digits during crashes. And, if that is possible as it is now, then there is no need to buy into speculations while the best of breed in Brazil is trading for such attractive valuations.

Strengths

Brazil has massive reserves of oil and natural resources. It is a democratic country with transparent political and economic systems (for an emerging market). It is a strong and welcome player on the world stage and will play host to the upcoming Olympics in 2016 and World Cup Soccer in 2014. Brazil boasts a huge tourism industry. It is a creditor nation with exports greater than imports. It is energy independent, has a huge population, second only to the United States in the Americas, and a functioning and transparent stock exchange. Brazil has enjoyed strong sustained growth during the past five years, entering recession only once for two quarters during the U.S. financial crisis.

Weaknesses

While transparent, the government has been known to hide spending on social programs under other categories of spending or not declare them altogether. There is a history of out-of-control government spending, something that has been brought under control for now. Brazil has a history of extremely high inflation, well into the triple digits on an annual basis, as recently as the 1990s. Its strong currency is putting pressure on exports. Massive poverty still exists in the country, and is especially evident in the slums of Rio.

Opportunities

China is a massive importer of Brazilian natural resources. Investment into high-tech/medical tech/biotech could make Brazil the Silicon Valley of South America. An exporter of energy, Brazil is still exploring within its shores and could emerge a top global player over the next two decades if its deepwater drilling program pans out. It has a chance to be a model for emerging market growth in Latin/South America as a major populated country. Sao Paulo is emerging as South America's financial capital. If the rest of the Americas grows, Brazil, with its current stability, currency, and strong export sector, will benefit.

Threats

An overheating economy could cause interest rates to soar to combat inflation, which would bring growth to a dead stop. Political transparency could be better in terms of disclosing where the government is spending money. If it turns out the government is indeed funneling money to far left social programs, it could torpedo the ruling party. Global economic contraction, especially in China, could hurt Brazil the most of any emerging market as it is reliant on exports and natural resources for a good chunk of its growth.

11

Chile

A DIAMOND IN SOUTH AMERICA'S ROUGH

Chile has reformed its markets as well as any emerging nation. From its days as a despotic military-ruled basket case in the 1970s and '80s, Chile has emerged as a small but stable player in South America. Inflation, once rampant, is under control. A pro-business government has paved the way for strong commercial enterprise in this resource-rich country. But Chile is a one-horse town when it comes to investing.

Granted, it has the usual commercial enterprises such as banks, retailers, airlines, and tourism. But, it's a small country and its biggest asset by far is its natural resources, specifically copper. Revenues from copper make up fully one-third of the government's revenue and with the boom in global construction in the 2000 to 2007 period, Chile was in the sweet spot. Even today, with copper trading at levels well above those in the 1990s, Chile has shown 5 percent-plus GDP growth—amazing considering the major earthquake/tsunami that struck the country in 2010.

Known for a stable banking system and sporting South America's top sovereign debt rating, Chile has been able to balance its economic system through its rainy day fund, something rare in emerging markets of any size. The country maintains a sovereign wealth fund that has over $20 billion in assets, and the country continues to add to this investment fund in times when copper prices are high. When demand drops or during times of recession, the fund's capital, which is kept separate from the central bank reserves, can be deployed for stimulus purposes. The size of the fund is very small in nominal terms, but relative to Chilean GDP the fund makes up more than 10 percent of current annual output. It would be like the United States having an extra US$1.5 trillion lying around in non-debt capital to deploy.

Investing in Chile is not for the fainthearted. Like all emerging markets, the Chilean markets are relatively illiquid by U.S. standards and outsized returns or losses are the norm. There are a few individual stocks that deserve to be mentioned. Specifically, LAN Airlines (NYSE:LFL), Chile's airline, has a solid route system throughout the country and the region, particularly in Peru and Argentina, and also operates a cargo business. Vina Concho y Toro (NYSE:VCO) is major bottler and marketer of premium Chilean wines. South American wines are making strong headway into the global markets, and this company is a pure play on that industry.

A more diversified investment can be made through the MSCI Chile Investable Market Index Fund, which tracks 35 companies that trade on the Chilean exchange. It trades on the NYSE under the symbol ECH. Liquidity is quite good with several hundred thousand shares traded daily. The fund has good diversification with about 20 percent devoted to utilities, 20 percent to industrials, and 20 percent to materials.

One particularly good closed-end fund is the Aberdeen Chile Fund (NYSE:CH), which has returned more than 18 percent on average over the 10-year period ending in December 2010. It offers good diversification and a small dividend. However, it does not always trade at a discount to net asset value (NAV). Most closed-end funds that trade in small emerging countries and offer limited investment choices tend to trade at premiums—the price you pay for entry into a small market. However, even this fund trades at a discount periodically, especially when there is a crash in copper prices. But, unlike the 25 percent-plus discount rule I espouse for buying closed-end funds for countries like China, if you are able to buy into the Aberdeen Chile Fund at a discount between 10 and 15 percent,

Table 11.1   Portfolio Composition

	Percent of Net Assets
Materials	23.3
Financials	19.7
Industrials	19.1
Consumer staples	12.5
Utilities	10.4
Consumer discretionary	9.6
Information technology	3.7
Telecommunications services	1.1
Cash	0.6

Source: www.aberdeench.com/aam.nsf/usClosedCh/
announcements.

consider it a job well done. As of July 31, 2011, the portfolio was invested as shown in Table 11.1.

The Reality of Chile Now

Chile holds a special place in my heart. It is where both of my daughters, Isabel and Gabriela, were born. Having spent some time in the country, I have come to admire the fortitude of the Chileans to overcome all manner of crises from bloody coups and dictatorships to massive natural catastrophes like the magnitude 8.8 earthquake that struck the country in 2010, and emerge as one of the region's healthiest economies with a predictable trajectory.

My first visit to Chile was in the mid-1990s. I remember clearly the November day in 1995. It was memorable because I was trying to get a visa for my daughter to leave Chile and the U.S. government had just shut down operations worldwide as a result of the lack of passage of a budget. This caused embassies and consulates worldwide to close down. It took some intervention from a congressman in Maryland to resolve the visa dilemma.

Chile in the mid-1990s was still recovering from the 17 years of military rule under Augusto Pinochet, the Chilean general who seized power after the coup against President Allende in 1973. Evidence of the coup can still be seen in the form of pockmarks from bullets on the walls of La Moneda Palace (Mint Palace) in downtown Santiago. The country was reviving itself under the presidency of Eduardo Frei and instituting economic and free trade policies that would finally help lift the country out of economic despair and into the twentieth century.

Socially, the country was suffering from widespread poverty, not the type one sees in Nicaragua but an economic malaise that permeated the streets. People were not destitute but most were far from wealthy. A country of just 13 million people, Chile was a natural resource powerhouse waiting to be tapped. A few hours into our visit, one of the members of our group was mugged by a knife-wielding Mapuche in broad daylight just steps from the Plaza de Armas, the main square in town. It took a few seconds to sink in, but the message was clear. Below the surface, Chile still faced issues with its indigenous population.

Santiago is a beautiful city when the haze clears. I knew the Andes mountain range was around somewhere, but the pollution was so thick I could not see them. Finally, one day when I was on the 18th floor of a building, I was able to see over the thick haze and witness their magnificence. On the streets of Santiago crowds bustled into Mercedes buses that flew down the avenues spewing massive amounts of pollution with every push on their accelerators. The weather was crisp and cool as spring was coming to an end.

I did not know what to expect on my visit. I thought Chile to be a backward country with Spanish influence but not on the level of, let's say, Argentina. Tucked away on the Pacific Coast of South America, Chile is one of the longest and narrowest countries in the world. It has a huge coastline of some 2,700 miles while its width from the coast to the Andes averages just 109 miles. The country is so long that if you are in the north, you are in the Atacama Desert, the world's driest. In the midsection of the country you enjoy a Mediterranean climate and in the south, a rainy temperate climate. Chile's extreme south is one of the points of embarkation for journeys to Antarctica.

The Chilean landscape, especially in the southern lakes district of Los Lagos, is spectacular with large alpine lakes surrounded by snow-capped volcanos, the most beautiful of which is called Volcan Osorno, similar in appearance to Mt. Fuji in Japan. The southern part of Chile is also where you will find the biggest population of Mapuche Indians, indigenous inhabitants of the country. However, their population has dwindled, and they rarely frequent the major coastal cities except to visit the local markets.

One thing you'll notice right off the bat in Chile are people's names. While Spain was the major influence after its conquest of the region in the 1600s, you will discern the country's mixed European heritage evident in names like O'Higgins (Bernardo O'Higgins was an early leader) and that of my guide, Norman Jackson Concha. Those of pure Spanish descent look decidedly the same as persons you would see strolling the streets of Madrid or Barcelona, while mixed marriages over the centuries have produced a large population combining features of the Mapuche and Europeans.

Chile is a gastronomer's dream. The country has superb beef, so good that much of its prime beef is sold to the Japanese. It also has some of the best and widest varieties of seafood on the planet. Fresh seafood is abundant at the coastal markets and it's cheap and delicious. Chile is also a real estate gold mine if you don't mind the distance.

Vina del Mar

I sometimes have to chuckle when I hear about city comparisons. Take Vina del Mar, a beautiful coastal city north of Santiago. It is referred to locally as the San Francisco of Chile. Its sister city is Sausalito, just across the bay from San Francisco. While it is doubtless a prime tourist destination with many very good eateries, Vina's draw is its breathtaking views, with the ocean on one side and mountains on the other. Add to that its casino, restaurants, and relative safety and tranquility and it is easy to see why it is the summer destination for many of Santiago's wealthy residents and politicians. Chileans tend to have three destinations at their disposal for recreation: the ocean, the mountains, and the unspoiled countryside where many have summer ranches.

I bring up Vina in particular because it offers a very nice price point for those seeking to invest in a stable, clean country outside the United States or Europe. Oceanview condos in Vina start at the low US$200,000 level and rentals in town for a nice two-bedroom condo can be had for less than $800 per month. Vina's population is less than 300,000, and it's only a 90-minute drive from Santiago and a metro ride from the nearby port city of Valparaiso where many cruise ships dock. Valparaiso itself is another option if you are seeking a city with a more urbane population.

Vina is a very mature, developed market for residences, which means that if you are a little more adventurous, you can positively steal oceanfront property in many other parts of the country, especially in the south where you can buy entire islands in the Pacific if that is your preference. Chilean coastal travel is easy on excellent roads, and there are luxury buses that will transport you anywhere for a song. Airline service is also excellent, with airports dotting the major coastal cities and frequent service. Getting around cities is also inexpensive using public transport or taxis. Many people look to Brazil, Argentina, or Montevideo for property close to the ocean. Chile offers a better, more stable alternative in my opinion. Locating property is quite easy and many Chilean realtors are online with listings. Buying real estate in Chile and for all of Latin and South America requires a little more due diligence than in the States. Be sure to buy directly from the owner and be sure that your attorney conducts a thorough title search. If you are dealing with an agent on the phone, sight unseen, you can be sure he or she will tell you exactly what you want to hear, which is not necessarily the truth.

Shopping in Chile

Chile is a shopper's paradise if you are interested in leather and lapis. Shoe shops can be found on every corner, sometimes more than one. Leatherware include items from nearby Argentina as well as locally made products. In the suburbs of Santiago you will find modern malls and shopping centers like the one in Las Condes, called Alto Las Condes, a short subway ride from downtown. There, you will find shops selling shoes and leatherware at surprisingly competitive prices.

But the real bargains are locally made crafts, which can be bought at markets throughout the country. Items like handmade sweaters, hats, handicrafts, and even beautiful copper works are cheap and abundant. Prepare to bargain.

Perhaps the best buy of all is lapis lazuli. There are two places in the world where lapis is mined in enough quantity to be made into jewelry: Chile and Afghanistan. Unless you are a serious adventure traveler, I would suggest Chile. In Santiago, there is a neighborhood called Bellavista where all the lapis shops and factories are located. It is well worth a visit. You could pay for your entire trip to Chile with some choice purchases. Do some research and then go to town. The selection is amazing and very reasonable, downright cheap in some cases compared to what you would spend in other parts of the world. Whether it's a picture frame or a necklace or a massive carving, you will find it here. Remember, with lapis it all boils down to polish and color—the deeper the blue, the more expensive the stone, regardless of size.

Tourism

Getting to Santiago and around Chile is quite easy. Once in the country travel is cheap and options are abundant. In Santiago proper, taxis, the subway, and other public transport are abundant. Santiago also offers many parks and its main streets and plazas are pleasant and relatively safe for pedestrians. Just don't try to cross the main thoroughfares unless you are at a crosswalk with stoplights!

It is once you get outside Santiago that the true beauty of Chile can be explored. Over the years ecotourism has become a burgeoning business and with good reason. Chile is all about the water and the mountains. Inland there is plenty to explore around the foothills of the Andes, and as part of the Rim of Fire, Chile is home to more than 50 volcanoes, scattered throughout the country. The tallest is over 18,000 feet. Many are snowcapped and quite a few are active, with the last major eruption in 2011 when the Puyehue Volcano in southern Chile erupted after 50 years of dormancy. Eruptions and earthquakes are part of life in Chile. Most large population centers are near fault lines and the narrowness of the country means that volcanoes are usually not too far away, either. Earthquakes tend to be infrequent, but some major ones have occurred, and this fact should be kept in mind when considering that real estate purchase.

Chile is as long as the United States is wide. It offers everything from high desert to lakes, fjords, the oceans, mountains, and plains. It even offers the world's most isolated island population at Rapa Nui or Easter Island, a five-hour flight away and inhabited by Polynesians. The island is most famous for its *moai*, giant stone statues carved hundreds of years ago. The tallest is more than 33 feet and weighs some 82 tons. There are some 887 of them all over the small island, each transported to its location some 500 to 700 years ago.

Chile offers something for everyone and is still quite unexplored by Western tourists. That makes it both a relative bargain and uncrowded. As an emerging market, it offers opportunity to invest in both hard assets like real estate and also in the resource industry as a backdoor play on Asian growth. The government is fiscally responsible, and Chile occupies a place among Tier 1 emerging market countries with little likelihood of reverting to a military dictatorship or heading down a socialist path.

Strengths

The country has a solid banking system, stable currency, and monetary authority. It maintains a sovereign wealth fund that is kept outside the central bank. Chile has massive reserves of copper. It boasts strong GDP growth from both internal growth and exports. Chile has a huge coastline that benefits commerce and tourism. It has a stable government and strong social safety nets.

Weaknesses

Chile is a small country with limited investment opportunities. As a major exporter of natural resources such as copper, it is highly dependent on emerging market growth.

Opportunities

Growth can come from continued expansion of trade with Asia. Ecotourism is still in its infancy. Real estate is relatively cheap for coastal property.

Threats

Natural disasters. Chile sits in an area prone to earthquakes, tsunamis, and volcanic eruptions. While major population centers are not at risk from all of these threats, they are close enough to be affected by one of the three. Competition from countries like Peru, also a major resource-exporting nation, that are targeting Asia. Chile has a much more transparent and fluid economic engine, however.

CHAPTER 12

Africa

AFRICAN RENAISSANCE

A good friend of mine just returned from Kampala, the capital of Uganda. He said the casino in Kampala was hopping. But the patrons were not Ugandans, they were Chinese. In fact, many of the signs are in Chinese.

Africa is enjoying a selective boom of sorts as the Chinese are making their presence felt by financing mega natural-resource-related projects. However, the selectivity is not so much boom related as it is country specific. Many people, investors included, tend to view sub-Saharan Africa as one giant country. It's far from that. From the jungles of the Congo to the coastal cities of South Africa, the continent's population is quite diverse, and most of the countries share little in common other than ancestry. In the Congo, French is the language of commerce. In South Africa, one should have a grasp of Afrikaans and English. In the Ivory Coast, again, French is dominant. Most countries also have several distinct native languages. In Kenya, for example, Swahili is the local language, but the 800,000-strong Massai speak their own language, which is more closely related to that spoken by tribes in Tanzania. The ruling party for many years, the Kikuyu, who number some 6 million (about 20 percent of the population) speak a variation of the Bantu language. And, so it goes on this continent of more than 54 distinct countries and over 1 billion people. It also presents a difficult proposition for investors because few can navigate through the variety.

Earlier I spoke about the opportunity presented in North Africa after the fall of the age-old regimes in Libya, Egypt, and Tunisia. The best way to play the upcoming renaissance in the North African region is through Egypt, in my opinion, and I outlined the reasons why earlier.

South Africa is also relatively easy to analyze as it is far ahead of most African countries in terms of development. East Africa (Kenya, Uganda, and Tanzania) is also well developed, in an emerging market sense, as these countries have been explored and developed by European colonists for many, many decades. Smaller countries really have very little to offer from an investment point of view since many, like Somalia, barely offer their local populations opportunity, let alone foreigners. The West Coast of Africa offers pockets of opportunity, but many countries in the region are also not really suitable for inexperienced investors, nor experienced ones in many cases. My focus will be on the countries where opportunities exist, whether on the ground or through the stock market, either locally or through exchange-traded funds or mutual funds. It would be easy to have written Africa off in the past, but for the past decade the continent overall has been the second fastest emerging market growth story behind South America and even ahead of Asia. Granted, the starting point is very low and growth, while impressive, is not on the same total dollar scale as that of Asia or South America. Fifty percent growth in the past decade sounds impressive, but as my old statistics teacher used to say, numbers don't lie, people do. Africa's boom is narrow and in order to buy into it, you'll need nerves of steel and lots of hope. And, as the Chinese have discovered, lots and lots of patience, as well.

East Africa

I have yet to see a place as beautiful as East Africa. I know it well. I was born there. From the beautiful coastal cities of Kenya and Tanzania to the inland lake country of Uganda, there are few places that can compare in natural and abundant beauty. From the snow-peaked summit of Mt. Kilimanjaro, through the plains of the Serengeti, to the Tsavo and Amboseli national parks, and the shores of Lake Victoria, East Africa is teeming with life.

I was reminded of this on a recent trip to the Grand Tetons and Yellowstone with my daughters. I offered them a dollar for each different animal they spotted on our drive through the Teton National Park. It was a very cheap excursion. I remember driving through Tsavo with my parents on our way from Mombasa to Nairobi. It was not unusual to see tens of thousands of animals at any given time on the plains. And, if the herds were migrating, the numbers could multiply tenfold.

I was born in Mombasa, a coastal city that first appeared on the European map when Portuguese explorer Vasco da Gama stopped there in 1498. The Portuguese later sacked the city and ruled it until the mid-1600s. Situated on the Indian Ocean, Mombasa was and is an important port city that has played a major part in the subsequent colonization of Kenya by the Arabs and then the British, who were the last colonial power to rule Kenya until 1963, coincidentally the year I was born.

The Kenya I grew up in was far different from the one that exists today. It was better . . . though not necessarily for everyone. My family came to Kenya in the 1800s as traders and merchants, following the British from northern India. My father worked hard to build a business as a distributor for Mobil Oil in the coastal cities. I enjoyed a lifestyle that could only be described as the best that colonialism had to offer. Servants, a large estate home overlooking the Indian Ocean, nannies, private schools—the works. Of course, the price of all this luxury was the low cost of labor and the massive inequality between the local African population and that of the merchant class, which was made up mostly of Asians and Europeans. After gaining its independence from Britain, Kenya and East Africa in general began to exude a different atmosphere. While never personally endangered, I clearly recall the extra security we would hire after stories of marauding panga gangs made the rounds. A panga is a machete, and victims of the gangs were usually hacked to death. The Kenyan independence movement was a result, in part, of the efforts of the Mau Mau uprising (the letters are an acronym for a phrase that basically said Africa is for Africans and the foreigners should go back home). The Mau Mau movement was a violent movement of Kikuyu origin, which had as its goal the return of the lands to the native population. Parts of the violent strain continued to make waves after independence.

The first Kenyan president, Jomo Kenyatta, was a member of the Kikuyu tribe.

However, Kenya was a harmonious Eden compared to its neighbor Uganda. Uganda gained independence from Britain in 1962 in a more peaceful fashion than Kenya. A decade later, peace was not even in the Ugandan dictionary. In 1971, a military commander, Idi Amin Dada, seized power through a military coup. He turned the country upside down in a period of seven years, destroying every shred of commerce, human rights, and prosperity in the process. Shifting alliances from the West to those who opposed the West, like the U.S.S.R., Idi Amin went on a nationalist rampage that involved the expulsion of the Asian and European population and nationalization of all of their businesses and homesteads and any possessions that they could not physically carry out of the country on planes, by car, or by train. He destroyed Uganda's economy, and he was responsible for upward of 100,000 deaths and maybe as many as half a million of the local population in purges, power grabs, and ethnic cleansing. Only today has Uganda begun to recover in earnest from the stone age that Amin left the country in when he was ousted in 1978.

An excellent movie, *The Last King of Scotland*, depicts the life and times of Amin and his brutal rule quite accurately.

Tanzania shared a similar story to that of Kenya and Uganda, but less violent. It was ruled during the first part of the twentieth century by the Germans and then the British. It gained independence in 1961 and proceeded to ally itself with China and took a path toward communism and nationalism. The country went through a major period of economic contraction after nationalizing many independent businesses in the 1970s, and it was not until the 1990s that the country began to regain some footing after abandoning the communist/socialist path.

All three countries of East Africa have been courting their former residents, the very same Asians that they either booted out or made life uncomfortable for, hoping to entice them to return and to set up business ventures. Uganda has returned many properties and businesses the prior regimes had illegally confiscated. The Asians are returning, though most have since settled in Britain, Canada, and the United States, and are contributing to the rebirth of the respective economies. It's not the same, however, and following a recent trip to Mombasa by a family member, I was informed that power outages and food shortages for certain products are not unusual, and there are six families occupying the home I grew up in. Fortunately, the countries have embraced the capitalist path once again, and the future looks brighter today than it did 40 years ago.

Frontier Investing

All three East African countries offer stock exchanges that are friendly to foreign investors as long as the rules and regulations are understood. The Dar es Salaam exchange, in the capital of Tanzania, offers foreigners the opportunity to invest locally but limits foreign-owned share ownership. Foreigners have been investing in the Nairobi Stock Exchange for decades, and some foreign-based companies have maintained local listings for just as long. Uganda's exchange is relatively new but offers the ability to buy shares through appropriate channels. Be aware though, that each market is very small and price swings and currency volatility will impact returns significantly.

For more information on investing directly in these markets you can use the following links:

- Tanzania: www.tanzaniainvest.com/
- Kenya: www.nse.co.ke/
- Uganda: www.use.or.ug/index.php

There is not a large domestic investing population in any of the exchanges as compared to a developing market simply because the people are, for the most part, poor. There are only two classes in East Africa, the super rich and everyone else. A middle class is forming slowly and education in East Africa is quite good compared with other African countries. Long-standing ties to Britain have helped these countries develop much faster and in a more stable and understandable fashion than others in the region, despite the hiccups brought on by independence.

Each of the countries is looking hard for foreign investment—not only in the form of a stock market purchase but in areas like factories, agriculture, tourism, and infrastructure. It can be hugely profitable for active investors to look to these East African nations as relatively stable and attractive entry points to the continent.

The cost of living in each country, as you can imagine, is quite low. However, it is low for a native lifestyle. If you wish to replicate a lifestyle enjoyed in a place like the United States, it can be as expensive as back home. Land is cheap. Oceanfront property is abundant and also inexpensive depending on location.

The biggest concern is safety. While not as bad as some parts of Africa, safety in major cities like Nairobi can be of concern for foreigners. Corruption is still the rule of the day and around election season bloody violence is not unusual.

East Africa has potential, lots of it. But successful investors must possess a frontier mentality and the ability to hustle like the locals and deal with bloated and corrupt bureaucracies. In this respect, the region is no different from most in Africa, Asia, or South America when it comes to investing.

There are other ways to invest. These ways include exchange-traded funds and, in some cases, country funds. However, most of these funds are not specific to one country, which provides a lot of diversification but will not deliver the types of on-the-ground profits and opportunity that can be had if you're willing to hop on a plane and do some legwork. English is the official language for business in East Africa and communication is not an issue. The probability of these countries reverting to the types of governments that ruled in the 1970s and 1980s is not great, but political and tribal tensions are an issue and tend to mar many positive developments that are occurring. In terms of where to invest in order of safety, infrastructure, and general business environment, I would rank Kenya and Tanzania ahead of Uganda. Uganda suffered the most and has been the slowest to recover. At the end of the section on Africa, I will offer some more general funds and investment ideas that encompass more than just East Africa.

Fleeting Signs of Success

Will the real South Africa please stand up? No country in Africa comes close to South Africa in terms of having the infrastructure in place needed to succeed. When I first began writing about the country there were two plays that dominated the headlines. First, there was the South African utility company Eskom, which had bonds yielding over 15 percent in the early 1990s, and then there were the resource plays, which have long been the source of great wealth for South Africans lucky enough to own the sector.

In the film *Diamonds Are Forever*, there was a scene at a South African mine where workers smuggled diamonds out in cavities in their teeth. If caught, workers were not just terminated but also likely suffered physical punishment, as well. It was the 1970s after all, and apartheid was the order of the day. For younger readers not familiar with apartheid, it refers to the legal division of South African society by the ancestors of the colonialist Dutch Boers, on the basis of race. In other words, if you were a black South African, your life was hell.

After suffering decades of embargos, diplomatic pressure, violence, and global ridicule, the ruling National Party began formal negotiations to end apartheid and engage in national elections, open to all races, in 1990. The culmination of these negotiations occurred in 1994 when the African National Congress, under the leadership of the formerly jailed political prisoner Nelson Mandela, assumed power in the country. It's been less than two decades since that day and South Africa has come a long way in many respects, but it has also failed to deliver on much of its potential in other respects.

As expected, the period immediately after the end of apartheid was a difficult one as the country's inner core, which was controlled in monopolistic fashion by the white minority had to transition to a new process. Government was now multiracial, businesses had to change their practices, and many people left the country for fear of retribution.

What did not change, though, was the immense opportunity for making money in South Africa. But, the South Africans, unlike the Zimbabweans further north, did not illegally redistribute the property owned by nonblacks. In other words, the transition was smoother, relatively speaking, and this allowed for the former rulers, the minority population, to remain engaged in the commercial community. Still, some vestiges of apartheid still remain, and race relations can be strained and retribution still occurs.

In some cities, like the largest city, Johannesburg, violence is a fact of life. Much of it is not directed at anyone in particular, just a seemingly random daily occurrence in a country where poverty and class division are still the rule and not the exception. The economic freedoms that are more widely enjoyed by all since the demise of apartheid are still, for the most part, tilted toward the white population. While many are seeing an improvement in their circumstances, poverty is still a major challenge with more than 25 percent of the population living on the equivalent of less than $2 per day. Consider that the cost of living for a family of four to live a middle-class lifestyle in a Johannesburg suburb is between $2,000 and $3,000 per month, and you can imagine the tenuous relationship that can develop between those who have and those who don't. Income distribution is actually getting worse. In 1995, the white population was earning, on average, four times more than the black population. (The per capita average annual income of $10,000 is quite high by African and emerging market standards, however.) Today that number is approaching six times. After the fall of the National Party, a massive exodus took place. That has since reversed and whites are returning to the country.

South Africa relies heavily on its strong resource sector. The country produces 90 percent of the world's platinum and more than 40 percent of the world's gold. It's an export-dependent economy with a healthy trade balance. China is its biggest customer and also the biggest exporter of goods to South Africa, which makes sense as China is basically devouring the natural resources found in most of Africa.

Yet, the money made from most of the country's commerce finds its way onto the books of a relatively small number of companies, long established in the region. The internal economy is primarily service driven, a strange situation to be sure for an emerging market. It has to do with the fact that South Africa is less of a true emerging market in terms of growth and more like a mature market, as it has been an established commercial country with strong European ties for centuries. Fully 65 percent of the working population can be found in the services sector. That is not a good sign for the country's growth prospects vis-a-vis places like China and Vietnam where a greater percentage of the population is engaged in the manufacturing sector. South Africa also suffers from a high rate of unemployment. Almost 25 percent of the potential working population is unemployed. Part of the problem is the lack of skilled labor and poor government planning post apartheid.

With a strong resource sector buttressed by strong market prices and demand for commodities, South Africa should be posting growth far greater than the 2 percent-plus in the past couple of years. South Africa is an emerging market in the sense that it has a lot of growth potential and is in a fairly volatile region that is dependent on the agriculture, commodities, and tourism sectors. It lacks internal diversification and that could present a problem going forward.

South Africa is also facing several crises borne of its proximity to countries like Zimbabwe from which people are fleeing in droves after the failed policies of the despotic regime of Robert Mugabe have rendered the country economically unviable. On my desk sits a bank note from my travels, which speaks volumes about the problems in Zimbabwe (see Figure 12.1).

Hundreds of people are crossing the borders daily resulting in a massive refugee problem for a country already suffering from massive unemployment. Tensions are high and violence is common in a country that is now engaged in xenophobic behavior—something that comes as a bit of a surprise considering its history of overcoming major racial intolerance. South Africa is also facing a major health epidemic. Fully 11 percent of the population, over 5 million people, is infected by the HIV AIDS virus, straining an already poor health care system. The country also continues to suffer from racial disharmony, a holdover from the apartheid days. This is not surprising, but it has lead to perceived unsafe conditions for many visitors and foreign business people. It is not advisable to walk the streets of Johannesburg at night, regardless of the distance, without adequate security. The problem is less acute in the suburbs, but many of my colleagues and friends have said little to dispel the current perceptions.

Investing in South Africa

There are many listed companies of South African origin that are tradable by investors. The country boasts the continent's largest market and its currency, the rand, is among the most actively traded emerging market currencies. The rand is a volatile

Figure 12.1   Zimbabwe Currency

currency, but in recent years has endured stability and growth against the U.S. dollar appreciating by more than 90 percent since late 2001. In December 2001, the rand fell to its lowest level against the U.S. dollar, dropping to approximately 14 rand to 1 dollar. The decline was due to two factors. First, there was fear that the land grab in Zimbabwe would spread to South Africa and the events of September 11, 2001, decimated many emerging market currencies. In 2011, the rand had retraced all the way down to the 7 rand to 1 dollar level on the strength of both the South African economy and the weakness in the U.S. dollar on the world stage.

The easiest way to invest in South Africa is through the MSCI South Africa Index Fund (NYSE:EZA), which offers excellent diversification amongst several sectors. It is heavily weighted in resources and financials. Over the past five years the fund has returned an average of more than 11 percent per year aided by a whopping 38 percent return between June 2010 and June 2011, a time when markets like China actually fell in value. One of the main reasons is the country's heavily weighted resource sector. Table 12.1 lists the top 10 companies in the MSCI South Africa Index Fund.

As I mentioned earlier, South Africa produces an incredible 41 percent of the world's gold and fully 50 percent of all the gold

Table 12.1   Top Monthly Holdings as of 8/31/11

Name	% of Fund
Mtn Group Ltd.	12.28
Sasol Ltd.	9.26
Naspers Ltd.-N Shs	7.09
Anglogold Ashanti Ltd.	6.09
Standard Bank Group Ltd.	5.96
Impala Platinum Holdings Ltd.	4.56
Gold Fields Ltd.	4.23
Firstrand Ltd.	2.86
Remgro Ltd.	2.48
Sanlam Ltd.	2.45
Total	57.26

Source: http://us.ishares.com/product_info/fund/overview/EZA.htm.

above ground has come from a South African mine. It's a sad state of affairs when a nation that dominates in the production of high-end resources such as diamonds, gold, and platinum still has a massive health and poverty crisis. South African companies are doing better at making their employees wealthier through greater ownership in companies, but only because they have little choice in the matter. To make money as a minority, you have to pacify the majority, and that means allowing equity participation, something that was unthinkable 20 years ago.

One of the companies that offers such participation and is a major philanthropic player as well is Sasol (NYSE:SSL) an international integrated energy and chemicals company based in South Africa. The company is a huge conglomerate involved in everything from fuel refining to polymer technology, and it is one of the best run and most profitable local companies. The exchange-traded fund I mentioned above owns shares of Sasol, as well. Earnings and earnings per share increased at double-digit rates in 2011 on the back of a very strong energy market in the early part of the year and an even stronger market for the company's polymer division, which saw year-over-year growth of over 60 percent.

Sasol's share price will follow that of oil prices. It gives you strong exposure to the South African economy, the currency, and the energy sector and is a worthy addition to any portfolio at the right price. Over the past five years, that right price has been in the mid $20s to mid $30s.

South Africa also offers a host of gold mining companies for investors looking to the resource sector. The two largest are AngloGold Ashanti (NYSE:AU) and Gold Fields (NYSE:GFI). Both companies are multimillion-ounce gold producers and own mines with significant reserves. Ordinarily, and in the past, companies like AngloGold would have appeared at the top of the list in terms of producers and cost. But the cost of doing business in South Africa is the high cost per ounce of gold, which is well in excess of $600 per ounce—great when gold is trading at $1,800 per ounce or more but not so great compared to its competition, which produces the metal at costs in the mid $400 per ounce range. The only reason I would invest in AngloGold or Gold Fields would be as part of a global resource portfolio. As you can see in Table 12.1, both companies are well represented in the MSCI fund.

The Other South Africa

South Africa is known for many negative things: AIDS, apartheid, and violence in Johannesburg and the surrounding black townships. But, it is a land of immense beauty, as well, and it recently hosted the Soccer World Cup, which was incident free and a huge gold star for the country. It also boasts one of the most beautiful cities on Earth in Cape Town on the tip of the African continent at the Cape of Good Hope. It offers both mountainous terrain and coastal views and is a favorite destination for tourists and expatriates alike. Inland, the country boasts some of the best wildlife viewing on the continent at places like Kruger National Park, which offers the best infrastructure of any African game park and is a perfect place for do-it-yourself safaris.

> *The Oxford Club*, a newsletter for which I was the investment director in the 1990s, once offered a trip to South Africa that combined the luxury of the Rovos Rail (think Orient Express) and a stay at the private Mala Mala Game Preserve. It was one of the most talked about trips that we offered.
>
> www.malamala.com/
> www.rovos.com

South Africa is perhaps the country in sub-Saharan Africa with the most potential to succeed. It has excellent infrastructure, massive natural resources, a booming tourism sector, a tradable currency, a multicultural population, and a somewhat transparent government. The question remains whether the country can come to grips with issues like its past and, more urgently, issues surrounding its problems with AIDS and poverty. The country is wealthy enough to match many first-world countries if managed properly. For investors looking to diversify into Africa, South Africa needs to be part of that portfolio.

Guns and Chocolate

West Africa is a mess. Over 50 percent of the population lives on less than $1 per day. Economic growth in the region is less than 2.5 percent, while the population in the region is growing at almost the same rate. That type of population growth requires economic growth of almost triple where it is today. Of the 15-odd countries that make up the region, 9 of them have experienced war or conflict in the past 20 years. Today, five countries—Ivory Coast, Guinea-Bissau, Liberia, Nigeria, and Sierra Leone—are still experiencing conflict. Two of the countries, the Ivory Coast and Nigeria, have strong global economic drivers. Ivory Coast produces 43 percent of the world's cocoa and Nigeria is the world's 11th largest oil producer. Both countries are rife with conflict and although both have supremely viable goods for sale, the majority of their populations are poor.

Risky Business

I remember writing about the "Nigerian scam" in the early 1990s, long before it made it to *60 Minutes*. It was my introduction to the region and has always left a poor taste in my mouth.

Nigeria has huge amounts of resource wealth, an educated population, and a developed economy. Yet, there are few places on Earth that are more corrupt. The government not only turns a blind eye to the corruption, it virtually sanctions it. There have been dozens of instances of government officials either involved directly in banking schemes or allowing their names and titles to be used in the schemes to bilk foreigners of their savings.

The Nigerian scam is basically a numbers game. Prior to e-mail, a gullible recipient in Europe or the United States would receive a letter on what appeared to be formal government letterhead claiming that the letter writer has uncovered an error in a major transaction and, as a civil servant, he cannot by law take advantage of this error. So, he is soliciting your help. He would like you to send him your bank account information after which he will wire the funds to you so that you can both share in this windfall. Your share will be 30 percent for doing very little. In some cases, they request that you send them a good faith payment to cover costs. Of course, the scheme is meant to get your vital information after which they can access your account, or to get you to send them money. Or, they will send you an official looking letter inviting you to the country to verify the details, after which you can return and do the transaction. They even offer a phone number or to call you, which they *will* do, to explain the details over the phone. Of course, none of this will really happen. In the end they will either siphon the cash out of your account or, if you are unfortunate enough to actually travel to Nigeria, they will shake you down at the airport or soon after with threats of kidnap or violence unless more money is sent over. The Nigerian government is well aware of this scam, which is also known as the 419 Advance Fee program referring to the section of the Nigerian penal code (419) that covers banking fraud. You would think that no one would ever fall for such a con; you'd be mistaken. According to Ultrascan, a Dutch group that monitors this scam amongst others, victims lost more than $9 billion in 2009, with Americans handing over more than $2 billion of that (www .ultrascan-agi.com/public_html/html/public_research_reports.html).

Scams as elaborate as the 419 scam, which really preys on small businesses and charities that are hurting for cash, could not be possible without the aid of postal officials, banking officials, and government officials in Nigeria.

Nigeria's massive oil wealth and huge agricultural sector have not helped the majority of the population. Nepotism is the rule of the day in the government and a very small segment of the population benefits immensely from the export of oil. Ethnic strife and religious tensions are rife, and personal safety is an issue in the country. But, the biggest problem is the rampant corruption that requires payoffs and bribes to be factored in as costs of living and doing business. Foreign investors can invest in the volatile Nigerian Stock Exchange. But, despite its stellar performance on occasion, the risk here is both loss of capital to volatility and possibly loss of capital to fraud. This combination makes the country a lousy choice for even the most adventurous investor.

The Ivory Coast is a different story. A former French colony, the Ivory Coast was an economic powerhouse (by African standards) in the 1960s and 1970s. In the 1980s economic mismanagement and the collapse of world timber prices led to the country amassing massive foreign debts, which subsequently tanked the economy and the government. Conflicts then arose between rival groups leading to a civil war that has lasted for more than three decades with brief moments of respite. Reasons for fighting ranged from citizenship issues surrounding the elected president to land grabs, corruption, and ethnic rivalries. Whatever the reason, the country is still in the midst of a nascent recovery from the most recent conflict in 2010/2011.

The rest of West Africa is made up of poor countries for the most part, although some do have oil revenues and a couple are actually quite stable. Countries like Mauritania experienced growth approaching 20 percent in the middle of the last decade . . . but the GDP was less than what Warren Buffett and Bill Gates give to charity every year! However, outside of investments in land for agriculture, few opportunities exist in the emerging market investing sense. Difficulty in investing due to illiquid currencies, poor legal protection, and potential for physical harm really make this entire region one to avoid in the short-term and likely also for the foreseeable future.

One-Stop Shop

There is an investment fund that will give you actively managed exposure to Africa through investments in some quality companies. It's called the Nile Pan Africa Fund (NAFAX), which is available through any brokerage house.

It's a very small fund, with less than $12 million under management and carries a pretty stiff management fee—around 5 percent. The management fee is not unusual as it is a very specialized fund. As an actively managed fund it can give you better exposure to a volatile region without having to worry about trying to trade in individual markets and setting up several accounts in several countries and using a host of currencies—another reason for the higher fee.

You can find more information about the fund and its manager by visiting the fund's home page at www.nilefunds.com/NilePanAfricaOverview.html.

Your broker will likely have never heard of the fund, and it's not going to be what you will hear people talking about at cocktail parties. But, if you want to catch a very early trend with massive potential, you may want to throw some play money at this fund.

Strengths

People power—Africa has more than 1 billion people and while very poor for the most part, the continent is growing in economic power. Natural resources—the Chinese are active investors in Africa looking to exploit the continent's huge mineral resource base. Tourism—Africa's national parks are huge foreign-currency-earning powerhouses that have yet to be exploited fully. Regional powerhouses like South Africa and East Africa offer strong opportunities for investors looking for growth that exceeds that of most regions in the world. However, the old saying about "return of capital" as opposed to "return on capital" should dominate any investment decision.

Weaknesses

Ethnic strife is still quite common. Corruption is the rule of the day. Africa is not a country, and it would be a mistake to consider it as a single entity. North Africa is much more developed than any other part of the continent. Lack of transparency, poor legal protections, and weak financial and government institutions are significant barriers for investors.

Opportunities

The resource sector is massively underexploited.

Threats

The lack of confidence in individual governments continent-wide has made long-term investing decisions impossible. In North Africa, the Arab Spring of 2011 continues to sow uncertainty in the minds of investors. In West Africa, conflict and corruption sap confidence. In East Africa, ethnic rivalries could derail government efforts at reform in places like Kenya. South Africa faces massive issues with crime and corruption. These are all threats that can be overcome with government policies that do not favor a very small segment of the population—a problem that has not abated despite the intense violence and even genocide in several countries. Investing in Africa is not for the faint of heart, but if timed well, the returns can out-pace those of any other region in the world.

CHAPTER 13

Central America and Mexico

Central America has been emerging as long as I have been investing. That's not a particularly good thing. The big kahuna is Mexico by a long shot. Then you have various smaller republics, some of the banana variety, like Nicaragua, Honduras, Panama, El Salvador, and Costa Rica.

Central America, with the exception of Mexico, presents little in the way of investment opportunity from a stock investor's perspective. But, opportunity does exist, especially for real estate and for retirement. Retirement is an investment just as day-to-day living is an investment. What Central America offers is a way for Americans to be close to home while living in large expatriate communities for relatively low cost versus the United States.

Countries like Costa Rica and Panama offer the higher end of the scale for retirees, while places like Nicaragua and Honduras allow for a much less expensive lifestyle but with fewer amenities. El Salvador offers little in terms of established communities for retirees looking to replicate some semblance of life "back home."

Real estate is by far the biggest draw in these countries. Land is easily accessible and prime real estate is within reach of most middle class Americans willing to do some legwork. Gone are the days when you could buy an oceanfront lot for US$25,000 but lots of opportunity still exists for those willing to look in the $100,000 to $150,000 range for a complete home close to and maybe even on the ocean. The real estate crisis in the United States, combined with massive losses in the financial markets, has resulted in a glut of properties.

Retirement in many of the countries can be enjoyed quite reasonably when you consider cheap health care, cheap labor, and cheap food costs. In places like Nicaragua one can live very comfortably on less than US$1,500 per month and still maintain a lifestyle that involves activities. One development, Rancho Santana, about a three-hour drive from Managua, offers a private residential compound that is fully developed to American standards. It's a 2,700-acre property with two miles of coastline and comes with amenities such as a restaurant, clubhouse, and nearby shopping. Lots in the development today can be had for less than $50,000 with ocean views. Turnkey homes can be purchased or built for less than $200,000. You can get more information at www.ranchosantananicaragua.com/.

Here are examples of listings that were current at the time of printing:

Privacy and Ocean Views: Bella Vista section of Rancho Santana. Lot N-6
Now up for sale is this 1.1-acre site that is particularly attractive, not only because of the ocean views and beautiful sunsets, but because of its location. It sits well in front of the road and other lots providing added privacy. No neighbors on either side or in the front! Build your dream home and enjoy all the amenities Rancho Santana has available. Priced at $85,000 or best offer.

Great Ocean Views: Bella Vista section of Rancho Santana. Lot N-17
This beautiful building site is 5,569 m2 (approximately 1.25 acres); it has beautiful ocean views; water and electric are installed to the front of the site, and it is ready for your construction plans. Priced at $60,000. For more information contact the owner.

Amazing Coastal Views: Playa Dorado section of Rancho Santana. Lot E-8
This site has great panoramic sea views of coastline, beaches, valley, and sunsets. It is in close proximity to the beach, restaurant, and clubhouse. Price is $35,000.
These listings can be seen in full on the website.

It takes a certain type of individual to make an investment in property in Nicaragua and for that matter, anywhere in Central America. You must be the type who can stomach bouts of political risk, sometimes-poor infrastructure, overdevelopment, incorrect title searches, and the obvious cultural barriers. While an oceanfront lot for $40,000 sounds like a great bargain, and for many it is, there are other considerations. Places like Rancho Santana are more than happy to host you for a few days to give you a feel for what it is like to buy and live in the area. While most people fly into Managua to get to Rancho, a better bet is to fly into Liberia in Costa Rica and cross the border that way—it's shorter and prettier. If you have never been to Managua, I can only describe it as a pit. Just to give you a feel, I stay at the best hotel in town, the Intercontinental Managua, when I am visiting Nicaragua. It's in the center of town. Outside my window I had great views of a strip joint and a Texaco station. Nicaragua is the poorest country in Central America, torn apart by civil war in the 1980s and 1990s. It is safer today, but as an investor you must be prepared to always have an exit plan.

Costa Rica

Costa Rica is the destination of choice for more and more Americans every year. Beautiful coastlines, superb restaurants, low cost of living, and a great health care system are all attractions. But, in recent years, crime in places like San Jose has also picked up, and not crime of the petty variety. I have spoken to many people in recent years who have left Costa Rica, primarily San Jose, because they became disenchanted with the increasing level of criminal activity. However, once outside the capital, there are few places in Central America that can compare with the country for beauty and quality of life. That quality of life, while still relatively inexpensive by American and European standards, is not so cheap anymore.

Oceanfront lots can easily set you back more than $250,000 in the better locations. Inland and in the mountains, you can still pick up bargain condos for under $100,000 . . . but it's the ocean that everyone wants. It's not uncommon to see homes priced as high as you would find in some southeastern U.S. coastal communities, which makes one wonder about valuations. Of course, owning real estate in a foreign country like Costa Rica, which is the most stable of Latin American countries, does present the opportunity to diversify assets abroad. For now, however, Costa Rican real estate is overvalued and a correction is in the offing. Prices are coming down as overbuilding is taking its toll. A sample of properties in Costa Rica can be found here: http://propertiesincostarica.com/listings.html.

San Jose has one of the best airports I have been to in Central America. Besides the free high-speed Internet access, it is clean, modern, and easy to navigate. It's best, however, to stay in the outskirts when visiting and maybe just do a quick afternoon trip to explore some of its colonial history. Restaurants are found everywhere and the food, especially the fresh fruit, is incredible. Costa Rica also boasts a new cruise port, and that brings in a lot of tourists who want to navigate through the Panama Canal. The country offers little in the way of investment opportunity other than real estate.

Panama

Panama is the destination of choice of many seeking a stable destination with a more cosmopolitan air. My first visit there was a little shocking, however. The journey from Tocumen International Airport into the city was quite eye opening as we drove through what seemed like a never-ending shantytown. Once in town, we went to a great seafood restaurant that had guards with shotguns patrolling the parking lot. The shantytowns are still there, but there are fewer guards.

Panama has always been a sort of financial center of the lower Americas. Drug money found its way to Panamanian banks by the boatload during the reign of Manuel Noriega, the long-since ousted dictator. Nowadays Panama is still a major financial center, but the days of money laundering in the open have gone by the wayside and the dealings are less conspicuous. The influx of foreigners buying up properties, particularly condos, and moving there en masse has lent an air of respectability to the country. The economy has been booming and Panama offers a free-trade zone, the cash-generating canal, and, of course, oodles of waterfront real estate. Panama does have a reputation, as does Costa Rica to some extent, as a destination for those enamored of the sex trade . . . a Bangkok of the Americas of sorts, but without the Buddhas.

Real estate in Panama is also becoming pricey, but its stability, banking system, and ties to the United States have made it a popular place to invest offshore with less risk than the other countries in the region. As with the other Central American countries, Mexico excluded, Panama should be viewed strictly as a real estate investment destination.

Honduras

Honduras is an up-and-coming destination for those seeking a cheap retirement. It's not the easiest place to get to, but if you are looking for an alternative to Nicaragua with similar price points and a better atmosphere, Honduras is the place to go.

Honduras is one of the few places that are quite livable where you can buy an oceanfront home or condo for less than $150,000. You can find more information by visiting this site: www.viviun.com/Real_Estate/Honduras/.

A good friend of mine, Barbara Perriello, who also runs a company called Opportunity Travel, spends a lot of time in Honduras and has also been involved in a few real estate deals there. She is an excellent source for both information and the inside scoop in real time. You can contact her at www.opportunity-travel.com/.

If you are planning to invest in property in a Central American country, be sure to get an excellent real estate attorney. Do *not* take what the real estate agent has to say at face value. The legal systems and title verification systems are antiquated at best, especially if you are purchasing from a local and not in an established development. Know that the cost of building a home, while inexpensive if you use locally made products and construction techniques, can quickly get out of hand if your tastes run closer to what you are used to in the United States or Europe. For most people I know, purchasing a property in Central America is a second home or a future retirement home. It's also a way to get money out of the United States and diversify assets.

Central America in general is fairly safe. But, the region is prone to political instability and in some cases natural disasters. Living there is not for everybody. It requires the ability to adapt to a totally different type of lifestyle, sometimes isolated. Local residents are, for the most part, extremely friendly but also extremely poor, and that can sometimes lead to uncomfortable situations for people not used to seeing extreme poverty in the Western hemisphere. If you do your homework and work with the right contacts and definitely rent before you buy, you will likely find yourself among the growing crowd that has made Central America their home away from home.

The Thailand of the Americas

I have often felt that Thailand enjoyed its position as a perpetual emerging market. It's been one for as long as I can remember and the dress fits well. I feel similarly about Mexico. One would think that a country so close to the world's largest economy, for more than five decades now, would be a shining star. I mean, 50 years and still an emerging market by global standards? Mexico is a moneymaker for investors who have money to begin with. If not, then it's just another emerging market clinging to hopes of a better tomorrow for its people.

Mexico's problems stem from its elitist society, dysfunctional government, monopolistic business practices, and a massive drug trafficking problem. Ten years ago, you could have said the same thing, and 20 years ago, too. But, for all of its problems, the country does provide investors with opportunities in sectors such as real estate, telecom, and infrastructure.

Things are better today than 20 years ago for sure. Then, more than 20 percent of homes had bare earth floors; that number is less than 6 percent today. Nearly every household has a TV, but fewer have refrigerators. Annual per capita income for Mexicans tops US$10,000, putting the country in the top 60 in the world for income. China's less than half that amount and the United States is almost five times that amount. Yet, if you were to spend a week in China, you would feel it was much better off than Mexico. The Mexican government is not known for its ambitious public works projects. Wander just a few miles outside most cities and beside the major highway, you will find mainly dirt roads.

Most people who visit Mexico today end up at one of its resorts such as Playa del Carmen, Cancun, Acapulco, Cabo San Lucas, or Puerto Vallarta on the various coasts of the country. Some end up in the interior at places like Mexico City, but that's usually a jumping off point or for business. Others, looking to retire, end up inland at Lake Chapala near Guadalajara.

Dependency Issues

Mexico sends fully 80 percent of its exports to one country: the United States. Only China and Canada export more to the United States in total dollar terms. This makes Mexico a virtual dependent of the United States. The advent of the North American Free Trade Agreement in 1994 allowed Mexico to move up the economic ladder more quickly. Imports by the United States from Mexico have almost doubled in dollar value since 1994, and imports to Canada have doubled. Mexico sports a trillion-dollar economy, yet it is half the size of Brazil, a country that it once was ahead of. Much of Mexico's early wealth was derived from its huge oil reserves, which have been dwindling. New discoveries have shrunk due to poor technology and lack of spending on trying to find new reserves. Meanwhile, countries like Brazil have tripled their expected oil production thanks to new discoveries.

Mexico does have a wild card in energy, however. It has massive access to the Gulf of Mexico, an area of significant oil reserves. The problem has been the government's hold on Pemex, the Mexican oil company. It is a monopoly that is government owned and, as such, is subject to the whims of an inefficient government program on expansion. What the government needs to do is to privatize or semiprivatize Pemex, much like the Brazilians did with Petrobras, and allow the company to both modernize its drilling program and exploit offshore reserves. But that costs money, a lot of money, and the Mexican government does not have that— even more reason to float the company to the open market. As the second largest supplier of oil to the United States in the past decade, Mexico has an easy and needy client to its north.

One of the greatest criticisms I have of Mexico is the lack of economic foresight that has plagued government after government. Corruption in Mexico's government has few bounds. Perhaps the biggest problem that faces the government today is narco-trafficking, an issue that cannot be resolved until and unless the government purges its ranks of individuals who profit from this multibillion dollar industry. Local and federal employees are complicit in this booming industry and not until very recently has the entire Mexican state faced the reality of the problem as it has made front-page news with mass killings and violent executions of innocent civilians caught in the crossfire. The equation for these corrupt politicians is quite easy. Pad their pockets with millions in cash or subsist on a meager salary.

Mexico is quite a paradox economically. While more than 40 percent of its population lives in poverty, the world's richest man hails from within its borders. Carlos Slim Helu, a Mexican of Lebanese descent, has amassed a fortune of some U$75 billion as the chieftain of Mexico's telecommunication industry. Through his holdings of America Movil and Telmex (formerly a government-owned enterprise) Slim has near monopolistic control of Mexico's telecom, mobile, and landline industries. Real wealth in the country is concentrated in the hands of a few, like Slim, which gives Mexico a type of Russian oligarchical economic system. In Mexico, wealth and politics are quite comfortable bedfellows.

Buying Mexico

Besides the obvious real estate investment opportunity in a country very close to the United States, Mexico offers a wealth of market opportunities, as well. While tied to the fortunes of its richer neighbor to the north, Mexico also enjoys an enviable position as a country that straddles two major global economic regions—North America and South America—with access to both via land and sea, with ports on the Pacific and the Atlantic/Caribbean/Gulf of Mexico. It's a position that has yet to be exploited fully. Mexico can profit from the long-term stability offered by the United States and Canada, despite recent cyclical headwinds, and also participate in the emerging growth of South America.

One of the top plays in the region is CEMEX (NYSE:CX), a multibillion dollar company and the world's largest supplier of ready-mix concrete. For speculators, CEMEX may prove to be a major win in the years ahead. The shares have been decimated thanks to overexpansion at a time when the United States and much of the world were engaged in a building boom that lasted from 1995 to 2007. When real estate in the United States, Europe, and the Middle East crashed, so did CEMEX's share price, currently trading around

$3.50, down from almost $37 in 2007. Much of the decline can be traced to the company's heavy debt burden that was accumulated during the boom to fuel expansion into markets like Europe and the Middle East. If the company can withstand the real estate crash, it stands to be one of the bigger winners on the way out. A strong global distribution network and the very likely boom in construction that lays ahead for emerging markets could pave the way to triple-digit profits from this play. On the flipside, a protracted downturn or a crash in emerging markets would likely result in receivership for this Mexican giant—hence the label of "speculative."

Mexico offers a wide array of local market plays, as well. Telephony has always been an attractive sector thanks to the monopolistic nature of the country's telephone providers. The big player in mobile telephony is America Movil (NYSE:AMX), majority owned by Carlos Slim Helu. The company offers access not only to the vast Mexican market where it holds majority share, but also into the Latin and South American markets. While competition within Mexico is virtually nonexistent for America Movil, it does face stiff competition in places like Brazil, Argentina, and Chile. Still, it is a high-growth business and mobile and Internet telephony show little signs of going the way of fixed lines.

Perhaps the most steady investment play coming out of Mexico is that of shares of Wal-Mart de Mexico, a $28 billion company with over 220,000 employees in Mexico and Latin America. The company has been growing steadily since the early 1990s when it entered the space in a big way. Investors can trade it in the United States under the symbol WMMVY on the over-the-counter market.

Promises, Promises

Mexico should be the world's top emerging market story. It's not. It has every possible advantage in terms of proximity to growth; proximity to technology; outstanding topography; a generally good primary education system; strong linguistic and social ties to the Hispanic and Anglo world; a huge population of expatriates; a massive, young population base; and wealth in natural resources. Yet, the country can't seem to get its act together, preferring to endure the cycle of boom, bust, and bailouts that is the hallmark of poorly managed emerging markets. With over a trillion dollars in GDP, an accomplishment that puts it in the top 20 globally, one can't get away from the fact that a visit to Mexico is no different than a visit to a third-world country in Asia.

Mexico has not delivered on its promise, but that does not mean that it can't in the future. But, to get there from here, the country needs serious political reform, a serious plan to combat narco-terrorism, a plan to revitalize its flagging oil industry, and massive investment in education and social reforms that keep its residents within its borders. Mexico is in the enviable position of having an ideal location for trade with the world. Cheap labor, low environmental barriers, an excellent transportation infrastructure, great tourist locales, a friendly population—these are all foundations that can build the country into a powerhouse economy of Latin and South America, along the lines of Brazil (although Brazil also has its share of problems). The issue is leadership and apparently that is something than money can buy in Mexico . . . to its detriment.

Strengths

Location. The region's proximity to the world's single largest economic power—the United States—and its proximity to the biggest trade zone in the world—North and South America—are big advantages. The region has a young population, low cost of labor, and a strong tourism base. It is an attractive destination for retirees. It has strong cultural ties to the highest growth population group in the United States. Economies are dollarized for the most part making trade easy.

Weaknesses

The region is plagued by political weakness and widespread corruption. It has poor central planning, weak infrastructure, especially water purification, and inadequate education spending. Class-based systems are not discouraged. It is dependent on the United States for growth. There are pockets of high crime related to the drug trade. The region has a lack of investment opportunities not related to real estate or tourism.

Opportunities

The region is close to the world's single largest trade zone (North and South America). It has strong cultural and linguistic ties to a strong emerging market region in South America. Continued development of its tourism infrastructure bodes well. In the case of Mexico, continued growth in exports to emerging markets, further modernization of oil infrastructure, and exploration.

Threats

Political disintegration. Countries like Nicaragua could easily fall backward into dictatorial rule, which could impact the investor opinion of the region. Narco-terrorism in Mexico poses significant headline risk and could potentially destabilize the government. Deaths are measured in the thousands annually and gruesome images continue to dominate media reports. A protracted downturn in the U.S. economy would negatively impact all countries in the region. Lack of reform of Mexico's oligarchical economic system, which tends to favor a wealthy few, could lead to Russian-style anger and despair within the population base. Natural disaster could disable one or more countries for years as few in the region have the financial reserves required for a major rebuilding effort.

CHAPTER 14

Eastern Europe

AS THE EURO GOES . . .

Eastern Europe is being held hostage. Except it's not by communism anymore. Countries like the Czech Republic, Slovakia, Bulgaria, Poland, Romania, and Hungary were once dependent on the largesse of their neighbors to the East. Long gone are the days of Soviet meddling and social experimentation. Today these countries find themselves pretty much on their own. It hasn't been an easy transition, and, for the most part, these countries have muddled into somewhat functioning democracies. Now, however, the region faces a massive economic threat thanks to the sovereign debt crisis in Europe that began in 2010 in Ireland and then spread to Greece and then Portugal, Italy, and Spain. Regardless of the ultimate resolution, the effects will be felt in these weaker peripheral economies the most. And that will provide both crisis and opportunity.

A visit to a place like Prague in the Czech Republic will give you the impression that these markets are anything but emerging. I recall driving from the airport in Prague through miles of ugly Soviet-era apartment buildings wishing I'd never come. But, once in the old town, everything changed and I was amazed at the wonderland that lay at my feet, literally. The Mala Strana area (little or lesser side) of Prague was so named because of its position on the left bank of the Vltatava River. It's a walker's paradise with restricted vehicle traffic. You are surrounded by outstanding examples of Baroque architecture, huge squares, and beautiful galleries. Walking amidst the crowds of tourists and locals are wig-wearing touts proclaiming the various musical events for the evening. One can walk around Wenceslas Square; see the magnificent Prague Astronomical Clock, installed in 1410 in the Old Town Square; and marvel at the modernity that was Prague after the Middle Ages. A former seat of two Holy Roman emperors, an important city for the Austro-Hungarian Empire, and a landmark city of the Habsburg dynasty, Prague has played a central role in Europe for more than a thousand years.

After falling to the communists after World War II, Czechoslovakia, Bulgaria, Romania, Poland, and Hungary went from somewhat thriving countries to vassals of the U.S.S.R., isolated from the West by their Iron Curtain status. Once-thriving economic and cultural capitals like Prague, Budapest, and Warsaw were now Soviet factory towns and remained so until the late 1980s and early 1990s when the decline of the Soviet empire freed them from totalitarian control.

The road back was not easy and continues to be quite difficult in all the countries once hidden behind the Iron Curtain, especially outside the major cities.

From an investment point of view, the countries are probably best looked at as a group rather than individually. Their economic past was reliant on industry, factories, shipbuilding, automotive plants, and the like. These industries are less relevant today, as competition from Asia has made them dinosaurs. Politically and socially these countries had to reinvent themselves overnight, transitioning from central control to independent countries again. Consider the efforts required to rebuild. Governments needed to re-form, a banking system had to be developed, infrastructure needs had to be met, and agricultural reform had to take place. And, all the while economic subsidies from the former Soviet Union all but dried up. Each country had to embark on a process of privatization and a quest for hard currency. It is for these reasons these once-thriving European nations (for the most part) earned emerging market status.

In the period immediately following their newfound freedom, these emerging nations, especially Poland and Czechoslovakia, found themselves the low-cost producers in Europe, and many of the Western European countries shifted manufacturing production to these countries to benefit from favorable cost structures. However, as the '90s wore on it was clear that Asia would come to dominate industrial production as the rising costs of rebuilding Eastern European countries and their wont for a higher standard of living comparable to their neighbors reduced their attractiveness. And, as is often the case with newly formed countries, heavy deficit spending and the ensuing indebtedness put inflationary and currency pressures on their respective economies, another hallmark of emerging nations.

Today, these countries are still lower cost producers, but the skill set of the general population is not keeping up with the technological shifts that are taking place in the rest of the world. Outside of small pockets of success in places like the automotive sector in the Czech Republic and continued privatizations in Poland, the region is still suffering from the slowdown in European growth in general. For the most part, double-digit unemployment, public sector corruption, accelerating social service and health care costs, and a population with a lesser skill set make these countries much less attractive than their Asian, South American, and African counterparts.

Worse still is their proximity to Western Europe and the former Soviet republics. Europe is mired in a major recessionary environment brought on by the financial crisis of 2010/2011, and the former Soviet republics, Russia especially, are flush with both capacity and their own internal problems. Eastern Europe looks to be mired in a rut right now and when recovery arises, it looks to be in the form of rapid-fire boom-and-bust cycles that may provide trading opportunities but little to get excited about over the longer term.

The Positives

The region does enjoy excellent infrastructure compared to developing markets in Asia, for example. And, it shares a common European thread dating back many centuries. This can provide an interesting opportunity for those inclined to look to the area for real estate investments. Eastern Europe may become a retirement destination for Europeans much like Mexico is attractive to Americans looking for a low-cost and comfortable place to retire.

The region is chock full of natural beauty and during the global real estate boom, many resort-like towns were developed. Many of these projects remain sparsely occupied, especially in places like Bulgaria and the now lower prices are attracting investors and non-residents alike.

As cost of living in Western Europe continues to top that of any developed country in the world, middle-class residents may look to escape the high tax, high-cost areas of Europe while not venturing too far from home to enjoy a relatively upper-class lifestyle and potentially retirement. Europe is well served by a vast transportation network of rail lines and airports that make traveling relatively painless and quick, when everything is running as it should.

From a stock market point of view, it is easy to buy into a myriad of Eastern European funds. And while these should have a role in your portfolio, the role should be minor compared to the booming markets outside the region, which offer a much better risk-reward picture.

Strengths

Eastern Europe's proximity to Western Europe is a plus. It offers a lower-cost destination for manufacturing. It has a good infrastructure and mostly democratic governance systems. Eastern Europe is educationally superior to many emerging markets outside Europe. It is linguistically compatible to Western Europe and has strong historic ties.

Weaknesses

Many of the countries are still dealing with a post-Soviet factory/socialist mentality, especially members of the older generation. There are weak currencies, high unemployment, and a seeming inability to modernize quickly enough to stave off competition from Asia.

Opportunities

Tourism and real estate are promising. The region could become the cheaper alternative for many European retirees looking to stretch their euros.

Threats

Asian dominance in manufacturing. There are weak social safety nets. Popular uprisings are not uncommon during periods of economic upheaval. Problems in Western Europe can severely retard economic progress. Rampant corruption exists at all levels of government.

CHAPTER

15

Argentina

FOUNTAINS OF WEALTH

There used to be a saying "as rich as an Argentine." It was a dream that could easily have been reality for longer than the century during which it was true. Argentina was once second only to Great Britain in terms of wealth. That was a mere hundred years ago. Things changed rapidly in this country that once was the envy of not only South America but Europe and North America.

Argentina is an ideal country for money generation. It practically grows in the fields. The country is blessed with magnificent farmlands, mineral wealth, rivers, mountains, and natural ports on the Atlantic Ocean. Unfortunately, it's also a political minefield with governments that seem to pride themselves on competing for "who can be the most incompetent and corrupt regime" in the nation's history. Nepotism takes on a whole new meaning here as the current government is displaying. The current president, Cristina Kirchner is the widow of the prior president, Nestor Kirchner, who won the presidency with a whopping 22 percent of the votes cast after his opponent withdrew from the race.

Back in the late 1800s Argentina was literally minting money. Its economy was expanding on the back of mineral wealth and agriculture. It was too rich. And that resulted in massive waves of immigration. The wealth was controlled by a small group of elites and, as is usually the case, the rest of the population began to demand a share and a vote. At first, entitlement programs were small but sufficient to promote harmony. The elites, while also a minority, also controlled the political scene. This changed in the early 1900s when more liberal voting practices were enacted. The combination of population expansion, entitlement spending and voting dynamics changed the landscape of Argentina forever.

By the mid-1940s, the country was declining under the burden of massive entitlement spending. Then came the deathblow in the form of a government led by Juan Perón and his populist wife Eva. They embarked on a program to emasculate the middle classes and distribute their wealth and property to the poor through a program of welfare that would bankrupt the country completely. Of course, there were healthy doses of corruption that accelerated this process. Suffocating taxes, an overregulated business environment, and threats of government seizure of cash and property brought the Argentine era crashing to earth by the middle of the twentieth century.

After decades of mismanagement, dictatorships, purges, and coups, Argentina finally found its footing in the 1990s and began a steady climb higher . . . until it once again adopted a populist mantra and proceeded to go on a massive spending spree. The problem was that the monies were borrowed and when it came time to pay them back, Argentina defaulted on its debt and was forced to restructure once again. The other thing that remained constant was corruption, of course.

The Naked Eye

To the naked eye, everything looks calm, collected, and even sophisticated on the surface. Traipsing down one of the magnificent avenues in Buenos Aires in the springtime is very similar to doing so in Paris. Of all the South American cities I have visited, I would have to say that Buenos Aires is the city that all aspire to be. It boasts wide, Jacaranda-lined avenues, beautiful parks, outdoor cafes, and even a celebrated cemetery, the Recoleta Cemetery. The cemetery, home to the graves of many of Argentina's famous and infamous such as Eva Perón, is located in one of the most affluent neighborhoods, Recoleta, boasting some of the city's best restaurants and hotels. It's a gorgeous area and a spot you should consider staying in during a visit to Buenos Aires. Everything you need is a short walk away.

Sitting at an outdoor cafe, sipping coffee and watching the well-dressed and well-coiffed locals wandering past you might suspect that prosperity flows well these days from Argentine taps. The buildings in Buenos Aires are beautifully kept and the French architectural styling could fool you into thinking you were sitting at a cafe near the Hotel George V in the eighth arrondissement in Paris. The only thing missing is the smell of fresh baguettes and the French chatter.

Dig a little deeper, and talk to the locals and you'll see that the surface is truly barely skin-deep. There is massive dissatisfaction with the government among the merchant class. There is little that is pro-business about Argentina. It's still about entitlements for the have nots and deficit spending and finding ways to either tax those who "have" or change the laws just enough to make financial assets less appealing. As a result, Argentines do two things. First, they buy hard assets like land and buildings. And second, they convert their money from pesos to U.S. dollars at every opportunity. Buenos Aires is one of the few major cities in the world that I have been to where I can spend dollars as freely as pesos . . . maybe more so. In the recent past, the government has frozen bank accounts, introduced new pension laws that restrict investments by their owners to government-backed debt, devalued the currency . . . in short, done just about everything wrong economically that a government can do, yet the city and the country still thrives below the surface. It's a testament not only to the Argentines, but to the wonderful country that they love to live in and boast about despite it all. Argentina is a beautiful place.

Dirt . . . Not so Cheap

One of my friends, Doug Casey, is developing a major property in a place called Cafayate, in Salta Province, about a two-hour flight northwest of Buenos Aires. He's pouring millions of dollars into a home/hotel/golf course development aimed at an audience that appreciates the beauty of Argentina's countryside: its mountains, its dry air, and clean living. I mention Doug because he is one of the best emerging market investors that I know—he's been to every one of them, more than once. He's been around much longer than me and has been investing in places like Thailand long before it showed up on any analyst's screen. Doug has a lot of confidence in Argentine property values. Property is a popular theme for investing among foreigners. Argentina is also a more welcoming place for Europeans thanks to the influx of so many in the early and mid-1900s. Asia, another favorite of both Doug and me for property is a much tougher society to crack. If you are going to take a trip to Salta or Cafayate in particular, stay at the Patios de Cafayate, one of the most beautiful properties in the region. The hotel is reminiscent of the type that you would find in California's Napa region. Beware though . . . there is only one small airstrip in Cafayate, and the winds have to be just right to land. If they're not, the pilot will detour to Salta, a larger city about a two-and-a-half-hour car ride away. This in itself is not so bad. Salta is a pretty town and the drive from Salta to Cafayate is quite pleasant and scenic, with some spectacular rock formations along the way. One thing that I was extremely impressed with about Argentina in general was the road system. It's an easily navigable country and potholes are not an issue.

Another friend, the person who hired me to do what I do more than 20 years ago, Bill Bonner, is also a large landholder in Argentina. Bill owns property all over the world and has a knack for buying things early. He's still shopping for more land in Argentina. Esteban Rosberg, another friend, is developing vineyards in Mendoza. He also owns a well-rated boutique hotel in Buenos Aires called the Fierro. Once again, the theme here is not the stock market but hard assets.

Land prices here can vary significantly depending on location. However, it's still much cheaper here than say Napa or Sonoma or Paris. It's even cheaper than Miami or Denver, for that matter. But for South America, Argentina is near the top of the list if you are looking for prime property. That said, if you are interested in an alpine home site in a great location, look into Bariloche (San Carlos de Bariloche) in the foothills of the Andes, where one can be had for less than US$100,000. You can purchase a fully furnished, rentable home in this location for less than US$300,000. A similar spot in the Rockies would set you back three or four times that, at least.

During the last meltdown and Argentinean debt default, apartments in Buenos Aires could be had for much less than US$100,000 in fabulous locations. Deals can be had here if you wait for the right time. And, that right time occurs about every five years in Argentina. If there is one thing you can count on, it's economic crisis. The government is extremely corrupt and few outside the small ruling circle trust anything that happens behind closed doors. This lack of progress and continuation of failed policies that depend on debt issuance and taxation continue to create an unpopular situation for the business class. That will continue to put Argentina in the crosshairs of boom-and-bust cycles that occur more frequently.

A Future Powerhouse

If the country could get its act together politically and fiscally, Argentina could easily become the per capita powerhouse of South America for decades to come. It has excellent infrastructure in place. It has a level of sophistication in its major cities that just is not found in emerging markets. The fact that Argentina is still considered an emerging market should be a source of embarrassment to the population.

Fertile farmland and pastures of the Pampas, navigable rivers, spectacular tourist destinations like the Andes and Patagonia, large urban centers, strong cultural expositions . . . these are all hallmarks of a much more developed country. The country has just enough going for it to make it a worthwhile destination for some of your investment dollars. If the people I mentioned earlier are any guide, those dollars should be heading for real estate or other hard assets and not into the stock market or into bank accounts—regardless of the stated return. The past has shown that the government has no qualms when it comes to changing laws overnight or even finding new ways to part you and your money.

Estancia de Cafayate: www.laestanciadecafayate.com/index
    .php?Adv=61da

Hotel Fierro: www.fierrohotel.com/hotel-overview.html

Hotel Patios de Cafayate: www.patiosdecafayate.com/

Strengths

Location. Argentina borders many of the countries in South America. It has excellent ports, ocean access, river access, great roads, and a developed airport system throughout the country. The country has massive mineral deposits, rich farmland, a fairly educated and sophisticated population by South American standards, and a strong business class.

Weaknesses

The government. Argentina has high debt levels, inconsistent banking regulations, and a volatile economic and political climate. It is prone to periods of social unrest and there is a strong bent toward populism. Its debt default in 2002 is a dark cloud for the country as far as efforts to attract foreign capital are concerned.

Opportunities

Real estate and vineyards. Argentine wines, especially Malbecs, are becoming well known throughout the world and have an attractive price point.

Threats

The government. Corruption is rife and a major stumbling block for anyone banking on long-term success. The country has a weak banking system, a weak monetary system, and is prone to bouts of hyperinflation.

CONCLUSION

Investing in Emerging Market Stocks

Buying stocks in emerging markets has never been simpler. I recall when I first started investing in these markets. Buying shares in companies like Malaysia's Sime Darby or Indonesia's Semen Gresik required a number of phone calls, currency translations, and hefty commissions. But, it was worth it as few investors outside the local countries were buyers and, hence, there was the opportunity to buy long before many had access.

Today, many foreign stocks can be bought through traditional channels as U.S. banks have recognized the demand. Banks have issued depositary receipts (DR), which are a proxy for the shares traded overseas. DRs offer several benefits. They can trade in U.S. dollars if offered on U.S. exchanges, offer a market, pay dividends, and are tradable during market hours. Bank of New York Mellon is a great source for DR information as it is the largest sponsor of the program in the United States. However, there are things that you need to know about investing via DRs that will make the process easier.

If the DR trades on a U.S. exchange, it will say so on the list and will trade either on the New York Stock Exchange, the NASDAQ, the over-the-counter market, or Pink Sheets. If it trades on the NYSE or NASDAQ, a readily available real-time quote will be available. If it trades on the OTC or Pinks, you will have to get a quote from your broker. It's always a better idea to first get a quote from the local market if it is open and then convert the number to U.S. dollars before placing your order. If the market is closed, the pricing will be based on the previous market close, and you have to be more careful as the bid and offer will have a wider spread to take into account the closed market. This should not dissuade you, however, unless you are trading during a period of volatility. In that case, the spread will be much wider to take into account the possibility of a strong overnight move.

Other DRs trade in financial centers like London or Frankfurt. In such cases, and really in all cases, you need to make sure that you are buying the right security by using what is called a CUSIP number. This is like a unique bar code assigned to every security. Buying stocks that do not trade on any U.S. exchanges will require a call to your broker who will then call his foreign trading desk for a quote. It will cost more in commissions and you will have to pay attention to currency translation. It may also be harder to sell during times of high volatility simply because of the time delay from quote to execution.

The DR as noted below also has a ratio: DR to ORD. This ratio simply means that each DR represents X number of ordinary shares. Ordinary share is the term used for the share on the local exchange. If you are basing your price on the price of the local share, be sure to multiply or divide by the right number to equate the price to the DR.

The Pink Sheets

The Pink Sheets is an over-the-counter (OTC) exchange that is basically a listing of stocks and their prices by active market makers. These are companies that don't meet Securities and Exchange Commission (SEC) listing requirements. Now, there are some out and out fraudulent listings on the Pinks (they got their name from the color of the paper that the companies and quotes were listed on prior to the electronic market), but there are also some major companies like Nestlé listed on them, as well. While the SEC requires significant listing and regulatory disclosures, many companies like Nestlé believe that there are better places to spend financial resources for listing requirements, such as their home base. This market is often overlooked by investors looking for diversification into foreign securities.

Trading on the Pinks requires some level of due diligence, however. Volume is usually very low and price quotes are often incorrect as trading may not occur in some securities for days. It is critical that you get an accurate price quote before placing a trade. You can do this by looking up the shares on the local exchange and converting back to U.S. dollars. It may take a little bit of time, but it is well worth it for the diversification and exposure.

The Serious Emerging Market Investor

If you truly are seeking to both move some cash offshore and invest like a local in many of these markets, especially Asia, it pays to open a brokerage account offshore. Before doing so, be aware that the account and its holdings must be disclosed to the Internal Revenue Service (IRS). With the recent push toward anti-money laundering, terrorism tracking, and tax avoidance, the IRS has issued very strict guidelines and penalties regarding holding accounts offshore and their disclosure on your tax returns. It is *not* the responsibility of a foreign broker to do this for you, and in most cases they could not care less about what the IRS thinks and therefore it is incumbent on *you* to file the disclosures on your tax return. You can learn more about the disclosures and penalties for not disclosing here: www.irs.gov/newsroom/article/0,,id=210027,00.html.

I would caution you to not be scared off by this extra step. If you are a serious investor, this is not a big deal. Just declare your accounts and holdings. It is not illegal to have a foreign account or to trade foreign stocks on local exchanges. The extra time and effort are well worth it, as investing in securities not available to the average investor looking to trade just U.S.-listed stocks can be rewarding.

Going offshore does not mean writing a check or making numerous phone calls to execute a trade. To the contrary, it is a simple process to open and fund an account electronically. A colleague of mine, Jeff Opdyke, has written extensively about investing in emerging markets and penned a great article about opening an offshore account at Boom Securities, based out of Hong Kong, to invest in Asia. As you can see in the following excerpt it contains a wealth of information.

1. Who is Boom Securities and is the firm safe to deal with?

Boom has been around since 1997, being the first online trading firm in Asia.

Boom is fully licensed, regulated, and monitored by the various securities authorities in Hong Kong. And Hong Kong itself is a highly regulated securities market. It's considered one of the world's "developed markets," on par with the United States, London, Tokyo, and so forth.

Boom has a record of zero disciplinary or regulatory actions, according to Hong Kong's Securities & Futures Commission, the local equivalent of America's Securities and Exchange Commission. So the firm is safe to deal with.

Private investors in Boom include the founder of San Francisco-based investment banking firm WR Hambrecht & Co. And this past summer, Japanese financial services giant Monex Group bought Boom. So Boom is backed by some big players.

2. How do you open an account with Boom?

This is very easy. All you have to do is direct your Internet browser to www.boom.com. There, at the top of the homepage, you will see a lime-green button with the words "Open an Account" in red. Click on that button and follow the prompts.

You'll see that you can apply in person (if you happen to be in Hong Kong and want to stop by the office). Or, you can apply by mail; just print the account application form, fill it out, and send it to Boom.

The biggest hurdle in this process—and I use "hurdle" very loosely—is the requirement that you have a copy of your passport and a copy of a recent utility bill notarized.

This is commonplace around the world. Unless you are sitting in front of an account representative, the firm has no clue who you are or where you really live. A notarized copy of your passport is proof that you are who you say you are; and the notarized utility bill is proof that you are a U.S. resident and not a local who's pretending to live in the United States to evade local taxes.

Setting up your account will take, maybe, two weeks as you collect the necessary documents and get them to Hong Kong so Boom can open the account. Boom will alert you when the account is open, and at that point you can wire money into the account.

Don't worry about missing the trade recommendations I make during that period. Stocks don't always move immediately, so you'll still have the chance to get in. And if the shares do move quickly, they often retreat and regroup before marching higher again, so you'll have that opportunity as well to initiate your position.

3. Is wiring money overseas safe?

Yes; it's incredibly safe. And it's exceedingly simple.

International wire transfers have been around since 1974. They're how governments, major corporations, and the wealthy move money around the world quickly, efficiently, and safely.

The process is based on so-called SWIFT codes that accurately direct money from one financial institution to another. I've personally been wiring money overseas—to places like New Zealand, South Africa, Egypt, Romania . . . and Hong Kong—for years with no problems.

All you do is head to your local bank and tell them you want to wire money to your brokerage account in Hong Kong. You give the bank the wiring instructions that Boom provides. The process takes about 15 or 20 minutes, and the funds transfer itself will take two or three days, depending on the day of week you do it.

Essentially, the wiring instructions first send your money into Boom's primary account at HSBC Bank in Hong Kong, one of the world's largest multinational banks. From there, the instructions indicate your personal account, into which Boom will automatically sweep your funds.

Once the money is in your account, you're free to trade.

And if any hiccups do happen, you're fine. Your bank will give you an international wire transfer statement that indicates all the important data points regarding SWIFT codes and account numbers. That way, if your transfer somehow misfires—and it likely will not—you can easily trace the funds through your bank and have them returned to your account.

And if the misfire happens on Boom's end, you can scan a copy of the transfer statement and e-mail it to the firm's support team (service@boomhq.com) and they will unravel whatever kinks happen to exist.

4. How easy is it to trade through Boom?

Well, how easy is it to trade at Fidelity or E*Trade or Charles Schwab? I'm not asking that question to sound like a smart aleck, but to make the point that trading with Boom is identical to trading online with any brokerage firm in the United States.

(Continued)

(*Continued*)

You log in to your account (using your own unique username and password), and you place the trade through an online platform. Just as in the United States, the platform requires that you indicate the stock you want to buy, the number of shares you want to trade, and whatever limit price—if any—you want to impose on the trade.

And that's it.

Once you're a client, you can sign up for Boom InfoExpress, in which the firm e-mails you updates on companies in your portfolio. So, if you own shares of a particular company that announces a dividend or releases its latest financial report—or whatever—Boom sends you an e-mail with the information so that you remain informed about what's happening inside your portfolio.

The firm also sends out confirmations every time a dividend lands in your account and every time a trade is settled. Plus, at the end of each month, you receive a note alerting you that your account statement is ready for your perusal.

And, you can go online any time and see your portfolio. You can move funds between several different currencies, including the U.S. dollar, Hong Kong dollar, and the Chinese yuan, among others. You can place trades in 11 different stock markets from Japan to Australia.

Because Boom provides low-cost, online trading across all of Asia (and it's the *only* firm doing so), operating through Boom is simply easy.

That said, if you're still leery and you want to work up to the point where you feel comfortable operating from an overseas brokerage, you can do some of the trading here in the United States.

Another source for emerging markets ETFs is: http://etf.about
.com/od/foreignetfs/tp/List_Emerging_Markets_ETFs.htm.

Investing overseas is easy. It is more accessible than it has ever been, thanks to technology. But, if you are still not comfortable with actually going offshore with your cash, you can invest through a myriad of exchange-traded funds in the United States. The problem is that you will not be able to invest in specific ideas, rather more macro ideas spread across various countries. Also, as I mentioned throughout the book, you can use closed-end funds to achieve your goals and possibly at a discount to the underlying assets being held by the funds.

More information on closed-end funds is available on this website: www.closed-endfunds.com/.

A P P E N D I X

World Oil Consumption Chart

Country	Oil Consumption (bbl/day)
Afghanistan	5,000 (2009 est.)
Albania	36,000 (2009 est.)
Algeria	325,000 (2009 est.)
American Samoa	4,000 (2009 est.)
Angola	70,000 (2009 est.)
Antigua and Barbuda	5,000 (2009 est.)
Argentina	622,000 (2009 est.)
Armenia	49,000 (2009 est.)
Aruba	8,000 (2009 est.)
Australia	946,300 (2009 est.)
Austria	247,700 (2009 est.)
Azerbaijan	136,000 (2009 est.)
Bahamas, The	36,000 (2009 est.)
Bahrain	39,000 (2009 est.)
Bangladesh	82,340 (2010)
Barbados	9,000 (2009 est.)
Belarus	173,000 (2009 est.)
Belgium	608,200 (2009 est.)
Belize	7,000 (2009 est.)
Benin	23,000 (2009 est.)
Bermuda	5,000 (2009 est.)
Bhutan	1,000 (2009 est.)
Bolivia	31,070 (2010 est.)
Bosnia and Herzegovina	NA

(Continued)

(Continued)

Country	Oil Consumption (bbl/day)
Botswana	15,000 (2009 est.)
Brazil	2.46 million (2009 est.)
British Virgin Islands	1,000 (2009 est.)
Brunei	16,000 (2009 est.)
Bulgaria	125,000 (2009 est.)
Burkina Faso	9,000 (2009 est.)
Burma	42,000 (2009 est.)
Burundi	3,000 (2009 est.)
Cambodia	4,000 (2009 est.)
Cameroon	26,000 (2009 est.)
Canada	2.151 million (2009 est.)
Cape Verde	2,000 (2009 est.)
Cayman Islands	3,000 (2009 est.)
Central African Republic	2,000 (2009 est.)
Chad	1,000 (2009 est.)
Chile	277,000 (2009 est.)
China	8.2 million (2009 est.)
Colombia	288,000 (2009 est.)
Comoros	1,000 (2009 est.)
Congo, Democratic Republic of the	10,000 (2009 est.)
Congo, Republic of the	10,000 (2009 est.)
Cook Islands	1,000 (2009 est.)
Costa Rica	44,000 (2009 est.)
Cote d'Ivoire	24,000 (2009 est.)
Croatia	106,000 (2009 est.)
Cuba	169,000 (2009 est.)
Cyprus	59,000 (2009 est.)
Czech Republic	207,600 (2009 est.)
Denmark	166,500 (2009 est.)
Djibouti	12,000 (2009 est.)
Dominica	1,000 (2009 est.)
Dominican Republic	118,000 (2009 est.)
Ecuador	181,000 (2009 est.)
Egypt	683,000 (2009 est.)
El Salvador	46,000 (2009 est.)
Equatorial Guinea	1,000 (2009 est.)
Eritrea	5,000 (2009 est.)
Estonia	30,000 (2009 est.)

(Continued)

Country	Oil Consumption (bbl/day)
Ethiopia	38,000 (2009 est.)
European Union	13.63 million (2009 est.)
Falkland Islands (Islas Malvinas)	0 (2009 est.)
Faroe Islands	5,000 (2009 est.)
Fiji	11,000 (2009 est.)
Finland	206,200 (2009 est.)
France	1.875 million (2009 est.)
French Polynesia	7,000 (2009 est.)
Gabon	14,000 (2009 est.)
Gambia, The	2,000 (2009 est.)
Gaza Strip	see entry for West Bank
Georgia	13,000 (2009 est.)
Germany	2.437 million (2009 est.)
Ghana	57,000 (2009 est.)
Gibraltar	21,000 (2009 est.)
Greece	414,400 (2009 est.)
Greenland	4,000 (2009 est.)
Grenada	3,000 (2009 est.)
Guam	10,620 (2009 est.)
Guatemala	79,000 (2009 est.)
Guinea	9,000 (2009 est.)
Guinea-Bissau	3,000 (2009 est.)
Guyana	10,000 (2009 est.)
Haiti	12,000 (2009 est.)
Honduras	56,000 (2009 est.)
Hong Kong	418,200 (2010 est.)
Hungary	137,300 (2010 est.)
Iceland	18,900 (2009 est.)
India	2.98 million (2009 est.)
Indonesia	1.115 million (2009 est.)
Iran	1.809 million (2009 est.)
Iraq	687,000 (2009 est.)
Ireland	160,900 (2009 est.)
Israel	231,000 (2009 est.)
Italy	1.537 million (2009 est.)
Jamaica	77,000 (2009 est.)
Japan	4.363 million (2009 est.)

(Continued)

(Continued)

Country	Oil Consumption (bbl/day)
Jordan	108,000 (2009 est.)
Kazakhstan	241,000 (2009 est.)
Kenya	76,000 (2009 est.)
Kiribati	0
Korea, North	16,000 (2009 est.)
Korea, South	2.185 million (2010 est.)
Kosovo	NA
Kuwait	320,000 (2009 est.)
Kyrgyzstan	15,000 (2009 est.)
Laos	1,918 (2010 est.)
Latvia	40,000 (2009 est.)
Lebanon	90,000 (2009 est.)
Lesotho	2,000 (2009 est.)
Liberia	4,000 (2009 est.)
Libya	280,000 (2009 est.)
Lithuania	74,000 (2009 est.)
Luxembourg	50,720 (2009 est.)
Macau	6,490 (2010 est.)
Macedonia	18,200 (2010)
Madagascar	21,000 (2009 est.)
Malawi	8,000 (2009 est.)
Malaysia	536,000 (2009 est.)
Maldives	6,000 (2009 est.)
Mali	6,000 (2009 est.)
Malta	19,000 (2009 est.)
Mauritania	20,000 (2009 est.)
Mauritius	23,000 (2009 est.)
Mexico	2.078 million (2009 est.)
Moldova	19,000 (2009 est.)
Mongolia	16,000 (2009 est.)
Montenegro	5,000 (2009 est.)
Montserrat	1,000 (2009 est.)
Morocco	187,000 (2009 est.)
Mozambique	18,000 (2009 est.)
Namibia	22,000 (2009 est.)
Nauru	1,000 (2009 est.)
Nepal	18,000 (2009 est.)
Netherlands	922,800 (2009 est.)
New Caledonia	13,000 (2009 est.)

(Continued)

Country	Oil Consumption (bbl/day)
New Zealand	154,100 (2009 est.)
Nicaragua	29,000 (2009 est.)
Niger	6,000 (2009 est.)
Nigeria	280,000 (2009 est.)
Niue	0
Norway	204,100 (2009 est.)
Oman	84,000 (2009 est.)
Pakistan	373,000 (2009 est.)
Panama	93,000 (2009 est.)
Papua New Guinea	36,000 (2009 est.)
Paraguay	27,000 (2009 est.)
Peru	150,700 (2010 est.)
Philippines	307,200 (September 2010 est.)
Poland	545,400 (2009 est.)
Portugal	272,200 (2009 est.)
Puerto Rico	164,100 (2009 est.)
Qatar	142,000 (2009 est.)
Romania	214,000 (2009 est.)
Russia	2.74 million (2010 est.)
Rwanda	6,000 (2009 est.)
Saint Helena, Ascension, and Tristan da Cunha	0 (2009 est.)
Saint Kitts and Nevis	1,000 (2009 est.)
Saint Lucia	3,000 (2009 est.)
Saint Pierre and Miquelon	1,000 (2009 est.)
Saint Vincent and the Grenadines	2,000 (2009 est.)
Samoa	1,000 (2009 est.)
Sao Tome and Principe	1,000 (2009 est.)
Saudi Arabia	2.43 million (2009 est.)
Senegal	39,000 (2009 est.)
Serbia	90,000 (2009 est.)
Seychelles	7,000 (2009 est.)
Sierra Leone	9,000 (2009 est.)
Singapore	927,000 (2009 est.)
Slovakia	79,930 (2009 est.)
Slovenia	60,000 (2009 est.)
Solomon Islands	2,000 (2009 est.)

(Continued)

(Continued)

Country	Oil Consumption (bbl/day)
Somalia	5,000 (2009 est.)
South Africa	579,000 (2009 est.)
Spain	1.482 million (2009 est.)
Sri Lanka	90,000 (2009 est.)
Sudan	84,000 (2009 est.)
Suriname	14,000 (2009 est.)
Swaziland	4,000 (2009 est.)
Sweden	328,100 (2009 est.)
Switzerland	280,000 (2009 est.)
Syria	252,000 (2009 est.)
Taiwan	834,000 (2010 est.)
Tajikistan	38,000 (2009 est.)
Tanzania	34,000 (2009 est.)
Thailand	356,000 (2009 est.)
Timor-Leste	2,500 (2009 est.)
Togo	21,000 (2009 est.)
Tonga	1,000 (2009 est.)
Trinidad and Tobago	43,000 (2009 est.)
Tunisia	89,000 (2009 est.)
Turkey	579,500 (2009 est.)
Turkmenistan	120,000 (2009 est.)
Turks and Caicos Islands	NA
Uganda	13,000 (2009 est.)
Ukraine	348,000 (2009 est.)
United Arab Emirates	435,000 (2009 est.)
United Kingdom	1.669 million (2009 est.)
United States	18.69 million (2009 est.)
Uruguay	34,670 (November 2010 est.)
Uzbekistan	145,000 (2009 est.)
Vanuatu	1,000 (2009 est.)
Venezuela	740,000 (2009 est.)
Vietnam	311,400 (2010 est.)
Virgin Islands	88,820 (2009 est.)
West Bank	24,000 (2009 est.)
Western Sahara	2,000 (2009 est.)
World	82.78 million (2009 est.)
Yemen	155,000 (2009 est.)
Zambia	16,000 (2009 est.)
Zimbabwe	11,000 (2009 est.)

Additional Sources

There are several advisors/sources that you can follow for advice and recommendations on emerging market investments. These are individuals who are on the ground in these countries and not sitting behind a desk surfing on their iPads.

Emerging Markets
Chris Mayer, editor, *Capital and Crisis*
http://agorafinancial.com/author/chrismayer/

Emerging Markets
Alex Green, editor, *The New Frontier Trader*
www.investmentu.com/investment-experts/alex-green-
   archives.html

Emerging Markets—Asia
Marc Faber
http://new.gloomboomdoom.com/public/pSTD
   .cfm?pageSPS_ID=6000

Emerging Markets
Jeff Opdyke, editor, *Emerging Market Strategist*
http://sovereignsociety.com/meet-the-editors/

China
Keith Fitzgerald, Money Map Press
http://moneymappress.com/author/keithfitzgerald/

About the Author

Karim Rahemtulla has covered international markets and the global movements of money for more than 20 years. With an expertise in emerging markets, options trading, and energy, he's regarded as one of the country's foremost resource and developing world analysts. His focus is on finding opportunities "beyond the dollar" for investors looking to diversify their assets and lifestyle to include borderless investing. He began his career heading up an emerging markets letter with a primary focus on South America and developing Europe and Asia, traveling extensively and frequently to countries like Turkey and China long before they appeared on the radar screens of investors. His most recent research trips include a visit to Cyprus during its financial collapse, a visit to Egypt during and after the revolution, two visits to Turkey, and numerous other destinations, including Cambodia, Thailand, Malaysia, and Vietnam.

Educated in England, Canada, and the United States, Karim is fluent in several languages. His undergraduate studies were completed in Economics and Foreign Languages, and his graduate coursework was completed in Finance. Karim is also regarded as one of the country's foremost innovators in options trading, with strategies ranging from income to aggressive speculation. On such merits, he travels the world regularly, seeking out the best investment opportunities, and is a featured speaker at more than a dozen frontline conferences annually.

Index